FAITH THAT'S NOT BLIND

**A Brief Introduction to Contemporary Arguments
For the Existence of God**

J. Steve Miller

Published by Wisdom Creek Academic
(A Division of Wisdom Creek Press, LLC)
Acworth, GA 30101
www.wisdomcreekpress.com

Printed in the United States of America

Library of Congress Cataloging-in-Publication Data

Miller, J. Steve, author.
Faith that's not blind : a brief introduction to
contemporary arguments for the existence of God / J. Steve Miller.
pages cm
Includes bibliographical references and index.
ISBN 978-0-9883048-4-0

1. Religion--Philosophy. 2. Faith and reason.
3. Truth--Religious aspects. 4. Natural theology.
5. Theism.   I. Title.

BL51.M627 2016   210
QBI16-900014

ISBN: 978-0-9883048-4-0

Library of Congress Control Number: 2016910847

Cover Art: Carole Maugé-Lewis

Permissions for Photos and Graphics

Photo of Francis Collins: By Bill Branson, NIH - http://www.nih.gov/about/director/images/Collins_formal_300.jpg, Public Domain, https://commons.wikimedia.org/w/index.php?curid=7751027.

Photo of Ernest Hemingway: photographer not specified, owned by John F. Kennedy library [Public domain], via Wikimedia Commons.

Photo of William Lane Craig: By ReasonableFaith.org (Reasonable Faith Press Kit) [CC BY 3.0 (http://creativecommons.org/licenses/by/3.0)], via Wikimedia Commons.

Photo of Alvin Plantinga: By Flex at en.wikipedia [Public domain], via Wikimedia Commons.

Photo of C.S. Lewis Statue: By "Genvessel" [CC BY 2.0 (http://creativecommons.org/licenses/by/2.0)], via Wikimedia Commons.

Photo of Henry Schaefer: By Rzepa at English Wikipedia [Copyrighted free use, Public domain or Public domain], via Wikimedia Commons.

Photo of Albert Einstein: by Orren Jack Turner, Princeton, N.J. Modified with Photoshop by PM_Poon and later by Dantadd. [Public domain], via Wikimedia Commons.

Photo of Isaac Newton statue at Oxford University: By Andrew Gray (Own work) [GFDL (http://www.gnu.org/copyleft/fdl.html) or CC-BY-SA-3.0 (http://creativecommons.org/licenses/by-sa/3.0/)], via Wikimedia Commons.

Marilyn McCord Adams Photo: By Kaihsu Tai (own work, Kaihsu Tai) [GFDL (http://www.gnu.org/copyleft/fdl.html), CC-BY-SA-3.0 (http://creativecommons.org/licenses/by-sa/3.0/) or CC BY 2.5 (http://creativecommons.org/licenses/by/2.5)], via Wikimedia Commons.

Blaise Pascal photo of sculpture: Augustin Pajou [Public domain], via Wikimedia Commons.

Thomas Nagel picture: By en:User:Jmd442 [GFDL (http://www.gnu.org/copyleft/fdl.html), CC-BY-SA-3.0 (http://creativecommons.org/licenses/by-sa/3.0/) or CC BY-SA 2.5 (http://creativecommons.org/licenses/by-sa/2.5)], via Wikimedia Commons.

Photo of Michael Behe: by Campus Photo • Bryan Matluk (The Maine Campus Online) [GFDL (http://www.gnu.org/copyleft/fdl.html) or CC-BY-SA-3.0 (http://creativecommons.org/licenses/by-sa/3.0/)], via Wikimedia Commons.

Photo of Fred Hoyle Statue: Mark Hurn [CC BY-SA 2.0 (http://creativecommons.org/licenses/by-sa/2.0)], via Wikimedia Commons.

Augustine Photo of Painting: Philippe de Champaigne [Public domain], via Wikimedia Commons.

Picture of Gestalt Drawings: By Alan De Smet at English Wikipedia (Transferred from en.wikipedia

Table of Contents

Introduction for Teachers/Professors
(Students: Feel Free to Skip This Section!)

Discussing the God Question in a New Day

As an instructor of religious studies in a state university, I aspire to equip my students to intelligently research and critically evaluate religious issues and current controversies. In an increasingly global and diverse world, such skills are vital.[1]

Arguably the most basic issues in religion ("basic" as to their importance for understanding religious folk and forming our own worldviews) concern life after death and the existence of a Supernatural Being (or beings). Are religious people who believe in such entities ultimately deceived, or could they be onto something?[2]

I'm amazed that in some classes, particularly introductions to philosophy, the God issue is often glossed over or deemed unworthy of serious attention (if my perusal of current syllabi is any indication). One introduction to religion text dismisses the question of God's existence in a paragraph by noting that "we can speculate *ad infinitum*" about such matters.[3] But since when do we avoid controversial issues in academia? In economics, we could debate socialist versus free market economies forever, but surely that's no reason to avoid a subject so central to economics.

One popular introduction to philosophy text deals with the God question by summarizing David Hume's argument against miracles, without any mention of contemporary critiques of Hume or contemporary defenses of miracles. The next chapter moves on to other subjects. [4]

The implication of such introductions? Intellectual history has moved past the God question; let's find something more interesting to talk about.

As a student at the University of Georgia in the late 1970s, my "Introduction to Philosophy" professor assigned Bertrand Russell's speech/article "Why I Am Not a Christian," followed by no critique and no serious class discussion, implying that Russell probably got it right about God arguments being defunct. Other such introductory classes may allow a debate on God's existence, typically resulting in little more than a sharing of ignorance, since few students in such courses have studied philosophy of religion in depth.

Perhaps many of today's professors teaching introductory religion and philosophy are merely following the lead of their own college courses decades ago. Yet, today we find ourselves at a vastly different place in intellectual history. The Big Bang Theory has revolutionized cosmology, giving strong evidence that the universe (including time and space and matter) had a beginning. For many philosophers and scientists, this relatively new cosmology has religious implications. Logical positivism waned (if not died) in the second half of the 20th century, so that talk of God is no longer ruled out *a priori* as meaningless.

Hume's arguments concerning miracles have come under sustained attack, and not just by theists.[5] Near-death experiences (experienced by one out of 25 Americans)[6] and deathbed experiences (experienced by over 80 percent of the dying, according to a recent study)[7] are routinely discussed in medical journals. One in three Americans claim to have witnessed or experienced miracles.[8] Many of our students have first or second-hand acquaintance with such experiences, so that they're vitally interested in making sense of them from an academic perspective.

Add to these observations the renaissance of philosophy of religion that has occurred in the past few decades, relooking at the age old questions through the lenses of fresh research and new scientific models.[9] Philosopher Quentin Smith noted that by the turn of the century, Oxford University Press' catalogue listed "96 recently published books on the philosophy of religion," of which 94 advanced theism and only two featured a "both sides" format.[10] We live in fascinating times!

Adding interest and relevance to the God issue since the turn of the century is "The New Atheism," which some claim is one of the most evangelistic groups in social media. Thus, God debates pack out auditoriums at university after university and are viewed with great interest on YouTube.

There's no lack of interest in the God question on the part of my students.[11] What a great opportunity to allow my students to explore a vital issue as they refine their research and critical thinking skills!

Finally, in the interest of promoting tolerance and resisting stereotypes, I want my students to intelligently question the common assertion that religious believers are uninformed science resisters, who, if they just read Bertrand Russell and Richard

Dawkins, would know better. Are there informed, intelligent believers out there? If so, how do they defend their faith? Have students been adequately introduced to religion if they've failed to wrestle with these issues? I think not.

One Way to Approach the God Question

So how can we introduce students to this vital aspect of religion? While I don't wish the God issue to dominate my introductory class (there are many worthy subjects and issues to address, including an introduction to major religions), I like to dedicate five or six class sessions to the topic, including homework and a brief paper.

Readings: I have students read or view, in consecutive assignments, 1) Bertrand Russell's "Why I am Not a Christian," 2) a contemporary critique of Russell's article, 3) David Hume's "Of Miracles," asking students to try to write out Hume's line of argument and evaluate it (a challenging task), 4) chapter four in Richard Dawkins' *The God Delusion*, where he presents his argument against the existence of God, 5) biologist H. Allen Orr's critique of *The God Delusion* in the *New York Review of Books* 6) an intelligent theist vs. atheist debate (Search "The God Delusion Debate, Dawkins Versus Lennox)", and finally 6) read this book (free as a pdf on our online component, D2L/Brightspace. Request if from me at jstevemiller@gmail.com).

Written Reflections: Students write a couple of paragraphs of agree/disagree reflections on points of their choice after each assigned reading and upload their reflections to their dropboxes on D2L/Brightspace. I also allow time for candid discussion in each class following their readings. (I try not to allow any one worldview to dominate discussions. In my class of 40, I'm finding that most prefer to discuss in small groups before sharing with the entire class.)

To help them to think critically about each assignment, I instruct them in class how to take arguments to the "Doctor", abbreviated as D.R., which stands for "Data" and "Reasoning." We ask:

- "What **data** was the argument based upon? Was it sufficient to warrant his/her conclusion?"

- "What line of **reasoning** did he/she use? Was it valid to draw his/her conclusion?"

Students use the same approach to critique the present book.

Brief Paper: Their paper is a thousand words on either "Why I believe/don't believe", or on a specific topic of philosophy of religion (e.g., the problem of evil), to give them the opportunity to flex their emerging research and analytical muscles and put their thoughts on paper in clear and lively prose.

In this way, I've exposed students to both sides of this issue, allowed them to reflect upon it verbally and in writing, and provided them with suggestions for further reading, to pursue the topic further.

On Learning from My Students

My students rate each line of evidence on a scale of one to ten (see below) and turn their ratings in as a part of their written reflections. I tally up their responses. Interestingly, some students resonate with one argument, some with another, and there's no consensus as to which argument is the most or least persuasive. Hopefully, by reflecting upon their responses, you'll learn much about what your students believe, how they think about their beliefs, and what personal experiences might have influenced their beliefs.

A Note on Style and Tone

Since Bertrand Russell and Richard Dawkins didn't shy away from putting themselves into their writing by expressing their own feelings and relating personal experiences, I've chosen to do the same (minus demeaning sneers) rather than write in a completely detached manner. Hopefully, this approach will help to arrest and sustain student interest in arguments that can sometimes become quite tedious.

On Future Editions

As it stands, this book should provide a helpful introduction to the field. Thus, I'm putting it out there. But I want more feedback—from students, professors, and specialists in each line of argument—which I can use for revised editions. Obviously, if I were to include all points and counterpoints, the page count would swell to the thousands, thwarting my intention: a *brief* introduction to arguments forwarded by intelligent believers. But corrections, tighter arguments, and more authoritative

"For Further Study" sections won't necessarily bloat the document; so please send any candid input to jstevemiller@gmail.com.

Introduction for Students
(Students Start Here!)

Personal Introduction

I teach an introduction to religion course at a state university. I love it! Why? Because I've been utterly fascinated with exploring spiritual claims for the past 43 years, starting in my high school days. The past 50 years has seen a revival of interest in these issues in both academic and popular publications, so much so, that it's impossible to keep up fully with this specialized field of study. Nevertheless, I learn daily and welcome fresh ideas, both from my students and my continued study. (I learn so much from my students!) Today I'm as motivated as ever. I hope this passion comes through in my writing, motivating you a bit further toward a lifetime of passionate learning.

Is Faith by Its Very Nature Blind?

Popular atheist Richard Dawkins derides religious believers as "faith heads," repeatedly characterizing religion as a realm of faith which people accept blindly. He singles out the Christian religion as teaching children that "unquestioned faith is a virtue. You don't have to make the case for what you believe." Thus he defines faith as "belief without evidence"[1] and insists that there's "no evidence to support the God hypothesis."[2]

Yet, many of today's believers beg to differ, claiming that their religious views are founded upon evidence as opposed to a blind leap into the dark.[3] And apparently they represent more than a remote fringe of religious thought, since professional philosophy of religion journals are flourishing and established publishers keep churning out a vast array of apologetics* themed books. If nobody reads such works, then how do the publishers stay in business?

> *Apologetics = The intellectual defense of religious faith.

This paper introduces the evidential side of faith—a faith that's not blind—as currently formulated by intelligent believers.

A Scientist Begins His God Quest

Francis Collins (1950-)

Francis Collins is one of the premier scientists of our time. He led the Human Genome Project, one of mankind's most ambitious scientific accomplishments, producing a map of the entire DNA sequence of the human genome. He currently directs the United States government's *National Institutes of Health*.

The son of secular freethinkers, his own freethinking as a college freshman (as he followed the reasoning of some of his atheist acquaintances) led him first to agnosticism, and more gradually to atheism. By graduate school he had become bold in his atheism, routinely challenging religious acquaintances, discounting their beliefs as "sentimentality and outmoded superstition."[4]

Yet in his third year of medical school, a seriously ill patient asked him what he believed about God. He suddenly realized that that he'd never actually "considered the evidence for and against belief." While he'd heard and resonated with atheists' arguments, he had never actually taken the issues seriously enough to carefully and objectively consider intelligent people's arguments for God's existence.

According to Collins:

> "That moment haunted me for several days. Did I not consider myself a scientist? Does a scientist draw conclusions without considering the data? Could there be a more important question in all of human existence than 'Is there a God?' And yet there I found myself, with a combination of willful blindness and something that could only be properly described as

arrogance, having avoided any serious consideration that God might be a real possibility. Suddenly all my arguments seemed very thin....”[5]

So for the first time in his life, Collins embarked upon a sincere intellectual search for God, although he was quite confident that it would merely serve to reaffirm his atheism. To his surprise, his quest led him to belief in God.

Why Ask Ultimate Questions?

What drives Collins, and a host of other intelligent seekers, to contemplate such questions?

Perhaps it differs for each person. But many realize at some point that the God question and the afterlife question are surely the most important and foundational questions we could ever contemplate. After all, they inform our big view of life–our worldview–trickling down to influence our priorities, purposes, morals, relationships, and attitudes. It's no wonder that so many of the greatest minds through the millennia reflected deeply upon the God question and took the time to write out their thoughts.

But secondly, some realize that they've never given the question serious and sustained thought, open-mindedly reading the most profound thinkers on the key issues involving faith. How could we skip this step and consider ourselves even mildly informed, much less fancy ourselves to be avid seekers?[6]

Now it's tempting to dodge the God question by throwing up our hands and saying, “There are so many opinions out there about God that I'll just concern myself with practical things, like getting a job and making ends meet.” But those who dismiss the search altogether haven't *opted out* of choosing a worldview. Rather, they've *adopted* a worldview–concluding that either God is unknowable or that He doesn't matter–both of which have vast implications for making life's biggest decisions.

To me, the question seems inescapable. So whether you're exploring this question for the first time, or continuing to explore a question that's fascinated you for years, why not find yourself a comfortable thinking spot, minimize distractions, and join me in the ultimate quest!

Preliminary Matters

What I'm Doing and Not Doing

This book doesn't present full-blown arguments for the existence of God. Rather, it merely introduces the *types* of arguments that intelligent believers employ. Thus, each point isn't intended to be some kind of slam dunk argument. Neither do I try to list all counterarguments. Rather, each line of evidence aspires to provide a pithy summation of more extensive formulations, typically found in full-length books, which motivated seekers can pursue on their own. Think of this as a starting point, not an ending point.

Why This Approach?

Surely it's valuable to get a basic overview of this vast field before digging in. Otherwise, someone may read a passage from Thomas Aquinas defending the Cosmological Argument and Immanuel Kant defending the Moral Argument, disagree with both, and imagine that they've sufficiently considered intellectual defenses of theism.[7]

Since the arguments tend to build upon one another, after a student reads more widely in the field, he/she can return to this list to see how one line of argument impacts another. In other words, in such a vast field it's easy to become so immersed in one line of argument, that students can miss the forest by obsessing on a tree.

Also, please be aware that this list is far from exhaustive. I chose arguments that I run across often in my reading, and seem to me, at this point in my intellectual journey, to have some weight. (Hey, I'm still learning!)

Our Approach to the Evidence: Which Hypothesis Best Fits the Data?

Thinking like a scientist or lawyer, let's consider two competing hypotheses and then try to weigh each line of evidence to try to decide which hypothesis best explains the data.

Here are the two, broad, competing hypotheses:

- **The Naturalist Hypothesis**: Observed data is best explained by the natural universe being all there is. There is no *super*natural or spiritual reality or God.

- **The Super-Naturalist Hypothesis**: Observed data is best explained by the existence of something more than the natural universe, i.e., something *super*natural or spiritual–perhaps including a God.[8]

As in most scientific and evidential approaches, we're not looking for 100 percent logical certitude. In an academic setting (particularly in the sciences), we typically look for "sufficient evidence" or "compelling evidence" or "the hypothesis which best fits the data."

The Nature of a Cumulative Case: How Many Lines of Evidence Must be Compelling to Justify Adopting Supernaturalism?

Typically, my naturalist friends say that since they see satisfactory naturalistic explanations for most phenomena of life, they *assume* naturalism until an argument comes along with sufficient evidence to convince them otherwise.

This approach implies that one strong argument could suffice to cause a naturalist to shift positions. As Harvard Professor William James put it, "If you wish to upset the law that all crows are black, it is enough if you prove that one crow is white."[9] Applying this to our present question, "If you wish to upset the hypothesis that we live in a purely naturalistic universe, it is enough to find one line of argument that provides sufficient evidence that a supernatural realm exists."

Consider a court of law. A jury might totally dismiss 10 lines of evidence put forth by the prosecutor, but be convinced by one line of evidence (e.g., fingerprints on the gun, or a trustworthy eye-witness account) that the defendant was guilty. So even if you rank 16 of the below arguments as zeroes, a solid 8 (out of 10) on one line of evidence might indeed be sufficient to compel belief.

But add in a couple of arguments that have a value of 6 or 7, and these might combine to yield a final tally of 9. In this sense, by examining several arguments, some may build a cumulative case that's stronger than any one argument in isolation.

How to Get the Most Out of Your Reading

Tip #1: Strive for objectivity. Many studies show a strong tendency, in intellectual pursuits, to find what we want to find.[10] Thus, rather than objectively searching for truth, some will read these arguments to find fault, others to gather ammunition. If you're reading this to win an argument with your dorm friends, you're not objectively seeking. Remember Dr. Collins' story. Although as a freshman he considered himself to be sincerely seeking truth, latter reflection convinced him that he was merely attracted to arguments he wanted to believe.

Tip #2: To keep from skimming through and ending up with a blur of information, stop and think about each line of evidence. Drawing tentative conclusions requires not only reading, but reflection. To insure higher level reflection, ask yourself after reading a line of evidence, on a scale of 0 to 10, how convincing the evidence is to you. Anything under "5" may have some weight, but is less than convincing, leading you to prefer a naturalist interpretation of the evidence over a supernatural interpretation. A "5" would mean you can't make up your mind which hypothesis best fits the data, so that you remain agnostic on that point. Anything over "5" means that you feel the data weighs in favor of the supernatural hypothesis.

Of course, if these are your first reflections on these arguments, then your decisions will be very tentative in nature; but at least you can draw a tentative conclusion as to where you are in your intellectual journey.

Tip #3: You'll often find extended discussions in the endnotes, and a guide to further research in the appendixes.

More Than an Intellectual Exercise?

Although this book examines spiritual questions as a purely intellectual exercise, I should remind readers that many religious traditions insist that the intellectual part of the search is only one aspect—perhaps not even the most important aspect—of a true religious quest.

Some emphasize the value of sustained practices of prayer, meditation, reading religious texts, attending worship services, etc. Keep this in mind as you read a book that limits itself to the intellectual side of the quest.

Exhibit 1
Near-Death Experiences (NDEs)

A Near-Death Experience (NDE) Rocks a Physician's Worldview

If you want to know what happens after death, it makes sense to consult those who have experienced clinical death (no heartbeat, no breathing) and have been resuscitated. Did some of them report "going somewhere?" Did some report to be fully conscious in another realm, at a time when their brains should have been incapable of consciousness?

> ***Reductionist:** Believes that, at least in principle, we can obtain a complete understanding of a process or thing by reducing it to its most elemental naturalistic components.

A patient's near-death experience shook Dutch cardiologist Pim van Lommel's naturalistic and reductionist* worldview. He knew from his medical training that when a patient experiences clinical death, the brain can no longer support consciousness or lay down memories.

Yet one day when he was on duty, the warning alarms sent doctors and nurses scampering to a patient's room to try to revive him. They succeeded, much to the

delight of everyone in the room...except for one...the patient! He was clearly ticked that he'd been taken away from a vivid, conscious experience in paradise to return to his ailing body in a dreary hospital room.

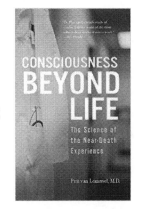

How could patients experience not only consciousness, but incredibly *vivid,* unforgettable, and life-changing consciousness, when their brains were severely compromised?

This dramatic event led Dr. van Lommel to embark upon a long-term study of NDE patients, eventually publishing the results in the prestigious medical journal, *The Lancet*.[1] Later, he published a full-length book on his findings.[2] He concluded that his former naturalistic view of life had been wrong. From his sifting of the evidence, he concluded that these patients actually left their bodies and experienced fully conscious life in another dimension.

Other Professional Studies of Near-Death Experiences

Dr. van Lommel was far from alone in his professional study of NDEs. In the 30 year period after Raymond Moody's 1975 publication of his seminal report on NDEs, *Life After Life*, 55 researchers or teams published at least 65 studies of over 3,500 NDEs. Prior to 2005, over 900 articles on NDEs were published in scholarly literature, gracing the pages of such varied journals as *Psychiatry* and *Critical Care Quarterly*. And NDEs aren't rare. About four percent of the populations of both the United States and Germany report having NDEs.[3]

Literature reviews (summarizing research findings to date) find patients who experienced clinical death reporting leaving their bodies and later reporting conversations and events (e.g., events in the hospital room) that others present at the time can verify. These aren't random dream sequences, as we'd expect from people who were semi-conscious. Rather, they are super vivid ("realer than real") and share common elements, such as leaving their bodies, finding themselves in a world where time and space seem to have disappeared, visiting with deceased relatives, talking to angelic beings, going through tunnels to reach a benevolent being of light, having their lives reviewed (often in full), discussing whether they should return or not, and finally returning to their bodies.[4]

Longitudinal studies find NDE patients remembering their experiences in accurate detail years later, and experiencing long-term life changes as a result.[5] These elements are remarkably consistent across cultural lines, typically counter to their expectations of life after death, making an explanation from psychological expectations a far stretch.[6]

Objection and Reply

Some object that the experiences could have occurred in the brief seconds that the brains were shutting down or cranking back up, or that minimal brain activity could have allowed them to overhear what was going on in the room. But remember: these are often extended (from the patient's perspective) experiences, sometimes reviewing their entire lives. And they are extremely vivid, laid down as an unforgettable memory, not like the vague recollections of dreams that are typically forgotten in minutes.

Consider the following case.

A Remarkable NDE

A patient underwent a risky brain surgery that required lowering her body temperature to about 50 degrees Fahrenheit and draining all the blood from her head. By three primary tests – a silent EEG, an unresponsive brain stem, and no blood flow through the brain – she was clinically dead. Yet, after the surgery the patient reported that she was very much alive during the surgery, viewing the procedure from outside her body.

She later described in accurate detail a conversation that transpired during the surgery and the specialized instruments used by the surgeons. Yet these events happened when her eyes were taped shut, she was deeply anesthetized, and 100-decible clicks assaulted her ears over 10 times per second to monitor her brain stem activity. Except for the small surgical area on her head, her entire body was covered.

Her ability to "see" and later describe the unusual instruments used in her surgery seem to fit with a worldview that allows for a mind to leave the body and view things without physical eyes. This doesn't seem to fit well with a naturalistic view that understands the mind to be purely a function of the brain, so that when the brain is shut down, the mind must shut down.[7]

The Broader Study

Decades of scientific investigation into thousands of NDEs reveals a phenomenon that's consistent with a belief in the afterlife, but seems inconsistent with the belief that death ends consciousness.[8] Supernatural elements include people blind from birth reporting seeing, the colorblind seeing colors, and communicating with relatives they didn't know had died. In other words, many who study NDEs claim that they're more than anecdotes; they're *corroborated* reports.[9]

Typical naturalistic explanations [such as the release of ketamine-like substances in the brain, psychological expectations, lack of oxygen (anoxia), the impact of administered medications] have been tested in various studies and found insufficient to fully explain the experience.[10]

At least twelve observations about NDEs seem to many to be consistent with a belief in the afterlife and God, but contrary to what we'd predict if NDEs were produced naturalistically, solely by the brain.[11]

Your Tentative Conclusion

At your current understanding of this line of evidence, how compelling (giving adequate evidence or reason enough for belief in the supernatural) is this line of argument to you? (Circle one number.)

Not convincing at all - 0 1 2 3 4 5 6 7 8 9 10 - Totally Convincing

To Continue Your Search

Since this experience is so widespread, why not ask your trusted friends and relatives if they've had such an experience? I was astounded to interview those in my circles of trusted relationships who had experienced NDEs. For further reading, start your research with a brief, but well-documented introduction: *Near-Death Experiences as Evidence for the Existence of God and Heaven*, which lays out the state of the evidence from secular scientific studies. It also recommends a course of further reading. If you want to read more of the NDE stories themselves, read the recent work, *Imagine Heaven*, by John Burke. Dr. van Lommel's book, *Consciousness Beyond Life*, is a very thorough examination of NDEs from a purely scientific viewpoint. For scholarly, peer-reviewed research, search "near-death experience" in the library or university databases. See especially the *Journal of Near-Death Studies*, 33 volumes, 1980s to present. The *International Association of Near-Death Studies* offers a comprehensive bibliography of over 900 articles (from 1877-2011) and select recommended books . The *Near-Death Experience Research Foundation* maintains a free online collection of over 4,000 NDEs in over 23 languages.

Exhibit 2
Deathbed Experiences

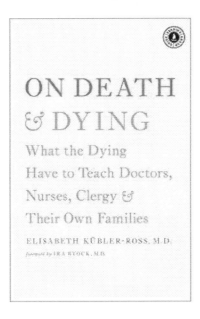

To discover if there's conscious existence after death, it makes sense to study the experiences of those who are nearing death. (*Near-death* experiences, by contrast, are typically experienced by people who come close to final death, but recover.) Perhaps there is evidence that they're making a transition to "the other side."

A recent study found the vast majority of dying patients reporting experiences with the other side that they claim are "more real than real,"[1] often involving conversations with the deceased – "typically vivid with great detail and personal meaning"–distinguishing them from typical dreams or hallucinations. Contrasted with delirium, these patients were characterized by "clear consciousness, heightened acuity, and awareness of their surroundings."[2]

But let's back up to look at a couple of seminal studies.

A Physicist Studies Deathbed Experiences

On the evening of January 12, 1924, Sir William Barrett, prominent British physicist and professor at Ireland's Royal College of Science, listened intently as his physician/wife shared excitedly about a patient, Doris, who was dying after she gave birth to her healthy child.

According to Lacy Barrett:

> Suddenly she looked eagerly towards one part of the room, a radiant smile illuminating her whole countenance. "Oh, lovely, lovely," she said. I asked, "What is lovely?" "What I *see*," she replied in low, intense tones. "What do you see?" "Lovely brightness—wonderful beings." It is difficult to describe the sense of reality conveyed by her intense absorption in the vision. Then— seeming to focus her attention more intently on one place for a moment— she exclaimed, almost with a kind of joyous cry "Why, it's Father! Oh, he's so glad I'm coming; he *is* so glad. It would be perfect if only W. (her husband) would come too."
>
> Her baby was brought for her to see. She looked at it with interest, and then said, "Do you think I ought to stay for baby's sake?" Then turning towards the vision again, she said, "I can't—I can't stay; if you could see what I do, you would know I can't stay."

Now many would conclude at this point that Doris was merely hallucinating. After all, nobody else could see what she was seeing. But what happened next threw a bit of a curve to the naturalistic hypothesis. Her sister, Vida, had died three weeks earlier, and everyone had kept the news from Doris in order to not upset her.

> On looking at the same place again, she said with a rather puzzled expression, "He has Vida with him," turning again to me saying, "Vida is with him." Then she said, "You do want me, Dad; I am coming."[3]

To the great physicist and his physician wife, both trained in the natural sciences, elements of this experience seemed to point beyond the natural, to the supernatural. Sir William was so intrigued that he sought out similar experiences, reflected upon them, and wrote about them in his book: *Death-bed Visions*.

If this were a purely naturalistic event, we'd assume that it would either be a random hallucination/dream or would conform to dying people's expectations of life after death. But the basic content of the "vision" is startlingly consistent across religious belief systems. And people generally weren't expecting the specifics of the experience. For example, in Barrett's study dying children were surprised that the angels they saw didn't have wings.[4]

A More Recent Study Using Modern Survey Methods

Inspired by Barrett's study, two academic researchers, Karlis Osis and Erlendur Haraldsson, both holding earned PhDs, determined to do a large-scale study of deathbed visions using modern scientific methods. They interviewed over 1,000 doctors and nurses about their experiences with 50,000 terminally ill patients. To control for the impact of expectations and cultural upbringing, they interviewed doctors and nurses in both the United States and on location in India.[5]

The researchers concluded that their findings conformed better to an afterlife hypothesis than a naturalistic hypothesis.

- The basic experience (seeing family members or religious figures coming to lead them into the afterlife) was largely the same, regardless of culture and religious background.

- Religious expectations concerning death were typically contrary to what they experienced, ruling out expectations as the cause of the experience.

- Naturalistic causes such as wish fulfillment, medical conditions, hallucinations, prescribed drugs, and lack of oxygen were considered but ruled out because of contrary evidence.

- The experience caused most of the subjects to desire death, in order to experience a much-improved afterlife. (If the experience had evolved through natural processes, such as adaptation and survival of the fittest, wouldn't natural selection prefer an experience that makes us fight for survival rather than give up the fight and prefer death?)

- The experience typically resulted in serenity, peace, and even elation at a time that we'd expect many to be racked with pain, distressed about leaving loved ones, and fearful of nearing death. It was as if they were separating from the concerns of this life and their body of pain.

- Sometimes they saw people on the other side that they didn't know had died.

- Often the patients were given a good prognosis and didn't appear to be near death; yet they spoke of a call to the other side and died shortly thereafter.

- Sometimes patients' brains had been losing function for some time, such as in cases of Alzheimer's. When seemingly comatose patients suddenly regain full consciousness and carry on animated conversations with deceased relatives, just before dying, this again seems unlikely under a naturalistic hypothesis.

- Those whose "vision" included a person who claimed to come to take them to the afterlife, died much sooner (87 percent of them died within the hour) than those who simply talked to people or saw a heavenly realm, but weren't asked to accompany them.[6]

Deathbed experiences aren't rare. According to contemporary researcher Christopher Kerr, they "are so frequent they are essentially intrinsic to the process of dying." In his 2015 study, he interviewed 63 dying patients on a regular basis and found over 80 percent reporting at least one deathbed experience.[7] This means that we can likely examine the data first-hand by interviewing friends and family and hospice nurses who have seen people die.

A Shared Death Experience Closer to Home

Sometimes living relatives share the visual and auditory transition with the dying person (called a "shared death experience".)[8]

One of my relatives, Bucky Barrett, (whom I have good reasons to trust for his sanity, intelligence, and integrity) had such a shared experience at the precise time of his father's death, 90 miles away, although everyone thought his father was in good health. Bucky reported that he woke in the middle of the night feeling a huge weight on his chest, left his body, saw a tunnel in the top corner of his bedroom, then returned to his body. He woke in a cold sweat to the ringing of his phone…a nurse telling him that his father had just died of a heart attack.

I share this personal experience to encourage readers to talk to their own friends and relatives about such experiences. Many will never share, unless they're "given permission" by someone they trust.

Your Tentative Conclusion

At your current understanding, how compelling (giving adequate evidence or reason enough for belief in the supernatural) is this line of argument to you? Circle one.

Not convincing at all - 0 1 2 3 4 5 6 7 8 9 10 - Totally Convincing

To Continue Your Search

On the shared death experience, see Raymond Moody's *Glimpses of Eternity: Sharing a Loved One's Passage from This Life to the Next*. Since deathbed experiences are so common, you may wish to ask your trusted friends and family members about such experiences. For scholarly, peer-reviewed research, search "deathbed experiences," "end-of-life experiences," and "end-of-life dreams and visions" in your library or university databases. For a recent literature review in a peer-reviewed journal, see "Deathbed phenomena reported by patients in palliative care: clinical opportunities and responses," by Devery, Rawlings, et. al., *International Journal of Palliative Nursing*, 2015, Vol. 21, No. 3, pp. 117-125. For a recent study in India, see Muthumana, Kumari, et. al., "Deathbed Visions from India: A Study of Family Observations in Northern Kerala," *Omega*, vol. 62 (2), pp. 97-109, 2010-2011.[17] Osis and Haraldsson's book gives an in depth look at their study. It's a bit academic, but well-written, including statistics, charts and objective measures rather than simply feel-good stories. It's titled *At the Hour of Death: A New Look at Evidence for Life after Death*, (White Crow Books: 2012). In this discussion board (as well as in a part 2), nurses are discussing deathbed experiences they've witnessed. http://allnurses.com/general-nursing-discussion/death-bed-visions-301825.html . Elisabeth Kubler-Ross was researching deathbed visions and near-death experiences in the same years that Moody did his original interviews. She wrote the influential book, *On Death and Dying*.

Exhibit 3
Contemporary Miracles and Answers to Prayer

Statue of C. S. Lewis (1898-1963) in Northern Ireland
Oxford and Cambridge Professor, Author of *Miracles*

Hemingway Solves a Very Personal Problem

The famous writer Ernest Hemingway lived out his adventurous, tough guy image—smoking, drinking, fishing the oceans, getting in brawls, fighting in wars, travelling the world, and attending bull fights. Once he even got out of his car to stare down a black bear that blocked his way (the bear left first). His writing often reflected his no nonsense, modernist, secular worldview. He just wasn't the churchy type.

But when he married his second wife, Pauline, he ran into a problem. A serious problem. He couldn't have sex. They tried everything to fix it, including consulting several doctors. Nothing worked.

Pauline suggested that he go to church and pray. According to Ernest,

Ernest Hemingway (1899-1961)
With his Family

> "Pauline was a very religious Catholic and I wasn't a religious anything,
> but she had been so damn good that I thought it was the least I could do
> for her. There was a small church two blocks from us and I went there
> and said a short prayer. Then I went back to our room…and we made love
> like we invented it. We never had any trouble again. That's when I
> became a Catholic."

Now Hemingway was no intellectual pushover. He knew modernist thought. He
read widely, in several languages. He associated with secular intellectuals. So
surely he explored every possible naturalistic angle. Perhaps acknowledging God
overcame some psychological barrier that was inhibiting his sex life. Perhaps his
trip to the church just happened to coincide with his body completing a needed
repair that was already in process.

But in his mind, those naturalistic options apparently seemed less probable than
a supernatural intervention. After exhausting every *natural* option to remedy the
problem, he had tried a *supernatural* option, and it worked. For Hemingway, the
most reasonable explanation was that there was indeed a God and that God had
answered his prayer.[1]

The Prevalence of Miracle Claims

Claims of the miraculous aren't rare. According to a recent Pew survey, thirty four percent of the population of the United States claims to have witnessed or experienced a miracle. That's about 300 million people–one in three Americans– who personally observed an event and believed that it was better explained as supernatural rather than natural.[2] Surely the serious seeker would want to critically investigate instances of claimed answers to prayer and miracles.

A Personal Approach to Evaluating Miracles

Some people (me included) tend to investigate such matters by diving immediately into the most respected books and peer-reviewed literature. But with so many eye witnesses to choose from, serious seekers should consider first-person research with their trusted friends and relatives. After all, there are many advantages to getting closer to your data. You don't have to trust other people's research, and you know whose testimonies to take with a grain of salt. (You can ignore Uncle Harry's claims, since last Thanksgiving he swore that Big Foot lives in his guest bedroom.)

So a holiday gathering of 12 relatives should, on average, yield four people who think they've witnessed a miracle. In such personal interviews with people I trust, some may have failed to sufficiently rule out likely naturalistic causes. Maybe it was an answer to prayer, maybe not. But from my interviews, some seem to have thought it through quite objectively, and concluded that a supernatural explanation makes the most sense in the light of the evidence.

My personal research (reading and personal interviews) convinces me that many events can be best explained as supernatural, consistent with divine intervention. These events are particularly compelling for those who personally experience them or have reports from trusted friends and relatives. Many have confirming documentation from doctors showing that that a naturalistic explanation was highly unlikely.

Objection

Of the many weird events that happen in life, a certain number will appear to be answers to prayer. Isn't it more intelligent to assume that there's a perfectly reasonable natural explanation that we've simply yet to discover?

Response

What you seem to be saying is that we should always assume naturalism. But why? The very question we're asking is, "Is there current evidence of supernatural events?" Now certainly future discoveries may explain away certain events that we now consider miraculous. But we can't very well import evidence from the future to help explain today's events.

Charges of "God of the Gaps" are well taken when used to explain events that are currently unexplainable by natural means, but in no way point to the supernatural. For example, I visited a Florida cave where the guide pointed to a spiral-shaped stalactite that scientists couldn't explain. Had I raised my hand and exclaimed, "then obviously, it must have been God!" this would be an example of randomly appealing to God to fill a gap in our knowledge. Similarly, some people in ages past attributed storms at sea to angry Gods, rather than assuming forthcoming naturalistic explanations.

But as Oxford philosopher of science John Lennox observes, while science fills some gaps, it opens others. When medical science tells us that a patient's advanced diagnosis is terminal, confirmed with tissue samples and scans, but a group of people pray and the healing is immediate, aren't we warranted to conclude that in all likelihood the prayer solved the problem, rather than assume that some naturalistic explanation is forthcoming? Dr. Craig Keener gives many such examples in his marvelously well-researched book, *Miracles*.[3]

A Personal Example

Once I began talking to people I trusted (they had no obvious ulterior motives for lying, like trying to sell books or urging me to join their religious group), I could begin to personally evaluate a sampling of the millions who testify to such things. Allow me to relate a personal example I recently heard from a family friend who was reluctant to share such things (many fear people will think they're crazy), but shared with our urging.

She had been in pain for some time with kidney stones. A doctor had done an ultrasound and determined that surgery was needed to remove them. They scheduled the surgery for the following Tuesday. Over the weekend, she attended church and after the service the wife of the speaker asked her if she could pray for her about anything. (At the time, our friend attended a church that didn't speak of miracles as being for today. Thus, she had no expectations that might invoke a placebo effect.)

Following the prayer, her pain subsided. When she saw the doctor for her Tuesday appointment, he did another scan to find precisely where to blast. The stones were inexplicably gone.

As John Lennox might say, science in this case strongly assured us that a natural cure wasn't forthcoming. 1) The stones were not going away on their own without a painful exit. 2) They were only going to get bigger and worse. Thus, the decision to schedule surgery.

Now you may say that it's more likely that the original scan was flawed or that a nurse eating a candy bar accidentally smudged the printed copy to make it look like a kidney stone. But if either of these were the case, then what was causing her pain and why did the pain disappear after the prayer? And what about the precise timing of the pain subsiding?

To me, in the case of my acquaintance, the timing of the prayer and the medical diagnosis lead me to believe that a naturalistic explanation is unlikely, and it's more likely that it was a divine intervention.

Beyond Personal Interviews

Dr. Craig Keener has done perhaps the most extensive research of our time on miracles. His scholarly, meticulously documented two volume set (titled *Miracles*) deals thoroughly with philosopher David Hume's objections, details scads of first-hand testimony to the reality of miracles, gives many examples of miracles that have corroborating features such as physician documentation and scans, and recommends many books by doctors and others who are in a position to evaluate such claims. He concludes that God indeed intervenes to heal and work miracles in today's world.

And as we said, reports of miracles aren't rare. They're alive and well globally. And they're persuasive to those who experience or witness them. According to one survey, "90 percent of new believers [in China] cite healing as a reason for their conversion."[4]

For Hemingway, this one line of evidence—his own healing—was enough to convince him that God is real. One college student told me that studying apologetic arguments helps her to talk to skeptics, but she didn't need such arguments to convince herself. Why? She claimed that she had seen too many miracles to doubt God's existence.

From what you know of miracles, how convincing are they to you?

Not convincing at all - 0 1 2 3 4 5 6 7 8 9 10 - Totally Convincing

To Continue Your Search

As I mentioned, the most exhaustive, scholarly, and recent study of miracles may be the two volume (over 1000 pages) *Miracles*, by Dr. Craig Keener. (See especially chapter 15, where he discusses the evidential value of various healings, and pp. 83-208, where he critiques David Hume's "Of Miracles"). It's extremely well documented and assesses not only specific miracles, but deals fairly with philosophical objections and scientific data. No study of miracles is complete without reading C.S. Lewis' reflections on the subject, again titled *Miracles.* For a skeptical view of miracles, read David Hume's essay, "Of Miracles," along with a good critique, such as Keener's *Miracles* (above) or *Hume's Abject Failure*, by prominent philosopher (not a theist) John Earman. Other books I've read with profit include *Remarkable Recovery*, by Hirshberg and Barasch, and *The Diary of George Mueller* (detailing a remarkable life of remarkable events, as he cared for and educated thousands of orphans in England.) Harvard Psychologist/Philosopher William James comments on Mueller's life in his respected book, *Varieties of Religious Experience* (pp. 361-371 on prayer).

Exhibit 4

Special Knowledge through Spiritual Encounters

In both near-death experiences and deathbed experiences, people claim to encounter spiritual beings *on the other side*. But what about those who claim to have encountered spiritual insight or beings on *this* side of life?

A Couple of Stories from My Circles of Trust

I have a relative who has a passion for fast. Although he has a Master's degree in history and taught history as his lifelong vocation, he loves to tinker with engines, pushing them to their limit by drag racing them. One day he was driving along a long, straight road, with no police in sight. He couldn't resist speeding up to over 100 mph. Suddenly, he heard a distinct voice from the back seat telling him, "Slow down." He looked back to ensure the back seat was empty.

Then he felt an uncomfortable tug on his shirt collar, like an irate mom getting a child's attention, and again heard, "Slow down!" He slowed down just before cresting a rise in the road that allowed him to see a fruit truck stalled in the right lane and an oncoming semi-truck in the other lane. Had he not slowed down, he would have almost certainly had to choose between crashing off the road or slamming into the fruit truck.

When I lived in Slovakia, a group of gypsies lifted my wife's wallet in the middle of a busy street and quickly headed through a breezeway to another street. Once Laurene realized what happened, she pursued them to retrieve her wallet (she was spunky in that way). But after emerging from the breezeway, a man dressed in white (unusual in the Slovak town) and speaking perfect English (even more unusual in 1993, just a couple of years after the fall of the Iron Curtain), warned her sternly that these gypsies were dangerous and that she should give up her pursuit. She once again looked forward, but when she looked back, he was gone. She was convinced that this was a visitation by an angel.

Looking critically at these two events, I know and trust both of these people for their integrity. Both are/were (Laurene is now deceased) intelligent and neither were prone to deceit or delusional thinking.

Since I trust their integrity and judgment, I can reasonably assume that I'd have drawn the same conclusion they did, had these events happened to me: a visitation by some spiritual being. So why wait for it to happen to me before assessing the weight of evidence?

But being a step removed, and naturally skeptical, I still assess their likelihood of being deceived in each case. In Laurene's case, I wasn't there to see the scope of her view. Sometimes people don't realize how long they look away before looking back. In this case, the "person in white" might have had time to walk out of view. But since I trust her judgment, I'll assume she probably took that option adequately into account and give the event a 6 out of 10, which puts me beyond an agnostic 5, even though the circumstances still give me some room for doubt.

In the other relative's case, hearing the distinct voice (not just a vague impression) and feeling a distinct tug at his collar, seems pretty objective. And then there's the timing. It's not like a person who might claim, "God told me to start this business and over the years it succeeded." In his case, the very moment after the voice and the tug, he crested the hill and saw the looming accident. And he's not prone to hearing voices. So I give his story a strong 8.

Now had this been a story I overheard from a pastor I didn't know, about a relative of his that I didn't know, I'd have to trust the veracity of both the pastor and the person it happened to, distancing me from the event and lowering its credibility. If I knew and trusted the pastor, depending on the nature of the story, I might still give it a 6. But if I didn't know him, and didn't know anyone to vouch for his integrity, I might give it a 1 or even a 0, since many speakers have a tendency to embellish their stories over time. Trusting a second-hand story is a different world from trusting a strong eye-witness account from someone I trust.

Objection

"Those stories have evidential weight to you because you know the people involved. But I don't know you (and whether to trust you); neither do I know them. So those stories have no evidential weight for me."

Response

Point well taken. But remember, this book merely introduces arguments and suggests ways to seek further. The point of these stories is to illustrate that a good *first step* in looking for miracles is to reflect on your own life, and then begin interviewing friends and family that you know and trust. Hearing their stories is much more persuasive than finding articles written by people you don't know, even if they're well documented or written up in a professional, peer-reviewed journal.

Second, beyond close friends and family, ask other acquaintances about their experiences.

Third, once we resort to stories of people we don't know, we must do due diligence to assess their integrity and their ability to assess the evidence. But even this third stage can yield strong evidence. In fact, as much as some people put down personal testimony, our courts of law would have to virtually close shop if they couldn't allow it in court and evaluate it. Juries (which by necessity of eliminating bias, don't personally know the accused) must assess the weight of personal testimonies of people they don't know every day in thousands of courts nationwide.

Evaluating Personal Testimony

The questions we ask in examining such stories are typically found in legal evidence. For example:

- Was it an eyewitness or secondhand account? (The further we get from eyewitnesses, the closer we get to hearsay.)

- Do we have reason to believe the witness is trustworthy in character?

- Does the witness have a motive for lying or exaggerating?

- Is it in the witnesses' best interest to *not* tell the event? If so, this bolsters their credibility. Think: a person testifying against the mob. (This is typically the experience of those telling their near-death experiences in a hospital setting. They're typically reluctant to tell their stories because they don't want people to think they're crazy.)

- How many witnesses were there?

- If we conclude that the claimed event happened, how plausible are suggested naturalistic explanations?

From your understanding of special knowledge and spiritual encounters, how do you rank them as evidence for the existence of God? (Circle one)

Not convincing at all - 0 1 2 3 4 5 6 7 8 9 10 - Totally Convincing

To Continue Your Search

While I see the benefits of keeping the research close by interviewing those we trust, much has been written on these encounters, but I've not sufficiently studied the literature to narrow down the best resources. One interesting account of special knowledge is related by academic neurologist Kevin Nelson, as he tries to give a purely naturalistic account of near-death experiences. A friend of Nelson woke in the night to the perceived presence (smells, the feel of her breath, 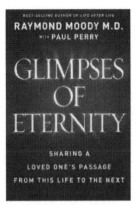 etc.) of his mother. He found later that she'd died that same night, "at that apparent moment," on another continent. Nelson tried to explain it away naturalistically by noting that the brain can produce sensations of smells. But to me, the remarkable timing, at such a remarkable distance, suggests that something of a spiritual nature triggered the experience. In Raymond Moody's terminology, it would be a "shared death experience."[1] Nelson's book is *The Spiritual Doorway in the Brain* (New York: Penguin, 2011), p. 148. Moody's book is *Glimpses of Eternity*.

Exhibit 5
The Beginning of the Universe

Dr. William Lane Craig (1949-)

Ultimately, where did the stuff (matter) of this universe come from? Here are the three main contenders:

1. Matter always existed.
2. Matter came to exist uncaused, naturalistically out of nothing.
3. Matter was created by something eternally existing outside of time and space.

Did I miss an option? If so, add it. Now, let's evaluate these options.

Concerning option #2, our consistent, overwhelming experience (scientific as well as personal) indicates that something can't come from nothing on its own. Not only do we have no experience of it happening, but it doesn't even seem to make sense. Effects demand not only causes, but *sufficient* causes. For me, this eliminates point #2 as a plausible option.

So let's look at option #1. Perhaps matter just always existed; it's just a bare fact that needs no further explanation. But philosophical evidence (the Cosmological argument) and scientific evidence (e.g., radiation from the Big Bang, the math of Einstein's Theory of Relativity, the Second Law of Thermodynamics) indicate that the universe had a beginning, before which there was no space, no time, no matter. Because of the present state of the scientific evidence, the Big Bang *is presently the reigning scientific theory of origins.*[1]

So if we eliminate options #1 and #2, we're left with option #3–that something pretty powerful and smart created matter–a Creator that sounds a lot like a God. The current state of science would seem to be consistent with the hypothesis that God, being eternal and existing outside space and time, created the universe out of nothing. A beginning out of nothing was not predicted by naturalistic scientists a century ago. Back then, the universe could have been explained as an eternally existing bare fact that needed no further explanation.[2]

Today's scientific view–that the universe came into being a finite time ago–begs us to produce possible explanations for the existence of the universe. Is it really plausible that something can come from nothing naturalistically, without the aid of Something that exists outside space and time?

The Kalam Cosmological Argument

Even if science one day shifts back to arguing that matter didn't start with the Big Bang, the cosmological argument argues that causes can't run back in time indefinitely, but must end in some kind of first cause–an uncaused cause. Otherwise you end up with an infinite number of past events, which seems to defy logic. Examples: If today's events were preceded by an infinite amount of seconds, then how would we have ever reached today? Or why didn't we reach this instant in time a thousand years ago, or a million?

Those who hold this "kalam" form of the cosmological argument argue that an "actual infinite" (an infinite amount of real objects or events or time) is impossible, or absurd. Of course, mathematics has ways to manipulate infinite sets, but it doesn't seem to make sense to make these sets refer to real objects, since we run into absurdities. Example: If an infinite amount of seconds preceded this present moment, then let's imagine taking away half of all the seconds. Absurdly, we'd still be left with an infinite amount of seconds. It simply doesn't seem to make sense. Time had to start somewhere, or we'd have never reached "now."

Scientific Findings that Confirm a Beginning for the Universe

The Second Law of Thermodynamics

This well-supported law seems to imply that the universe had a beginning. Since in closed systems (such as the universe), energy becomes more random and disorganized over time (called "entropy"), there must have been an initial time when energy was maximally organized. Thus, if the universe existed from eternity past, how could organized energy have lasted until today? At some time during an infinite past, the universe should have long ago run out of energy and all the stars (including our sun) should have grown cold.

Furthermore, if the universe's energy is winding down, how did it initially get wound up? Surely maximally organized energy didn't simply pop up out of nothing, naturalistically and uncaused.[3]

Big Bang Cosmology

Similarly, Big Bang cosmology tells us that the universe (including time and space) had a beginning. (Again, this is today's scientific consensus.)

Reflecting upon the Big Bang, where did the primeval atom—the infinitely dense point of energy that started it all—come from? Again, if science and observations have taught us anything, something can't come out of nothing without some serious help. As Maria sang in *The Sound of Music*, "Nothing comes from nothing, nothing ever could." Surely a spiritual being, existing outside time and space, would be a solid candidate for starting this whole operation going.

Objection

Some suggest that our universe may be merely one of many universes, collectively called a multi-verse.

Reply

First, we have no independent evidence of other universes, and theoretically we can't observe or test any such universes. Furthermore, a study by cosmologists Borde, Guth and Vilenkin argued persuasively (proving by working the math) that

> "Any universe which has, on average, been expanding throughout its history, cannot be eternal in the past, but must have an absolute beginning."

Thus, according to Vilenkin,

> "It is said that an argument is what convinces reasonable men and a proof is what it takes to convince even an unreasonable man. With the proof now in place, cosmologists can no longer hide behind the possibility of a past-eternal universe. There is no escape, they have to face the problem of a cosmic beginning."[4]

So at best, a multiverse theory seems to merely push the ultimate beginning back in time, failing to eliminate the need for a beginning.

Conclusions

Francis Collins concluded:

> "The Big Bang cries out for a divine explanation. It forces the conclusion that nature had a defined beginning. I cannot see how nature could have created itself. Only a supernatural force that is outside of space and time could have done that."[5]

Quantum chemist Henry Schaefer concluded:

> "A Creator must exist. The Big Bang ripples (April 1992) and subsequent scientific findings are clearly pointing to an *ex nihilo* [out of nothing] creation consistent with the first few verses of the book of Genesis."[6]

Interestingly, when PhD candidate Jana Harman studied conversions from atheism to theism in her dissertation, she found the number one argument that had a part in changing their minds involved the beginning of the universe.[7]

Not convincing at all - 0 1 2 3 4 5 6 7 8 9 10 - Totally Convincing

To Continue Your Search

Start with a an animated video found here: http://www.reasonablefaith.org/kalam . For a scholarly presentation of the Kalam Cosmological Argument, by today's most recognized proponent (by virtue of his debates, books, formal education and peer-reviewed publications) see *The Kalam Cosmological Argument*, by William Lane Craig, or one of his many debates. For a lay presentation of this argument, see chapters three and four of Craig's book, *On Guard*. For a more advanced discussion, see chapter three of Craig's *Reasonable Faith* (pp. 93-156). Here's a good blog post: (http://edwardfeser.blogspot.com/2011/07/so-you-think-you-understand.html) by philosopher Edward Feser, responding to common criticisms of Aquinas' version of the Cosmological Argument. The history of the Big Bang Theory and the second law of thermodynamics are relevant to this discussion as well, to see how naturalistic scientists fought against both and resisted their implications. For this history, see two exceptionally researched books by Helge Kragh: *Entropic Creation* (Ashgate, 2008) and *Cosmology and Controversy* (Princeton University Press, 1999).

Exhibit 6

Six Super-Precise Numbers
That Fine-Tune our Universe for Life

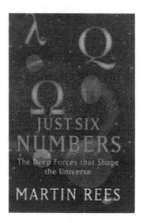

Our universe and planet have been described by scientists as existing in a "Goldilocks Zone"–not too hot, not too cold to sustain life. In fact, at least six numbers must have been set with extreme precision shortly after the Big Bang to allow for not only life, but the formation of matter, including stars and planets. Yet, the odds of these precise settings occurring by random chance are astronomical.

Example: The Strong Force that holds atoms together must be set at precisely 0.007. If it were set at 0.006, the universe would be nothing but hydrogen. If set at 0.008, there would be no hydrogen, and consequently, no water. Without this intricate setting, and at least five other precise numbers, life could have never developed. Yet, scientists (such as Richard Dawkins and Martin Reese) tell us that there's no reason why a universe must necessarily come pre-packaged with these settings.[1]

Oxford Physicist Roger Penrose estimated that the odds of the universe having just one of these six settings–its precise low entropy settings–are one chance in $10^{10^{(123)}}$ [2]

Thus, we must seemingly choose between an incredibly massive stroke of luck (required by naturalism) or a Designer (consistent with supernaturalism).[3]

Counterargument

Dawkins and Reese consider the two contending hypotheses (naturalistic and theistic) and suggest that perhaps ours wasn't the only universe created by the Big Bang. The multiverse theory suggests that a huge number of universes (perhaps infinite in number) might have been created by the Big Bang. If this occurred, then conceivably each universe would have different random settings and at least one of them (including ours), would have settings that allow for the formation of stars, planets, and life.

Reply

One problem with the multiverse theory is that there's no evidence for even one universe other than our own, much less a great multitude of universes. Perhaps it's consistent with (but not demanded by) String Theory, but String Theory itself seems to be based upon little hard evidence, and one astrophysicist told me that it's falling out of favor for this reason.[4] Thus Reese admits that his preference for the multiverse as an explanation, over positing God as the explanation, is "no more than a hunch."[5]

Some may respond that conjuring up a God is no better than conjuring up a multitude of universes, since He's supposedly invisible to us as well, out of reach of scientific investigation. But if readers find weight in any of the lines of argument in this paper, each argument provides corroborating evidence for an Intelligence capable of "setting the knobs" with precision. I don't find similar corroborating evidence for a multi-verse.

An Analogy

Imagine that you order a sound board for your band, set it up in your basement, and the next day you find the six digital knobs set up precisely (out of thousands of possible settings for each knob) as you prefer them for your band. Would you assume a naturalistic, chance reason for these settings? (Perhaps millions of these sound boards were produced, each with different settings, and you were lucky enough to get the one with the exact settings.) Or, would you assume personal agency? (A fellow band member came over when you weren't aware and adjusted the settings).

For me, personal agency seems a much more reasonable hypothesis, for both the sound board and for the universe.[6]

Not convincing at all - 0 1 2 3 4 5 6 7 8 9 10 - Totally Convincing

To Continue Your Search

From a secular standpoint, see Martin Reese, *Just Six Numbers: The Deep Forces that Shape the Universe*. From a theistic view, see William Craig, *Reasonable Faith*, pp. 157-172.

Dr. Craig refers to Dr. Robin Collins as "the finest exponent of the fine-tuning argument today."[7] (He holds PhDs in two fields that this argument intersects: Physics and Philosophy.) Find articles by Collins, both introductory and advanced, here: http://home.messiah.edu/~rcollins/ .

Dr. Luke Barnes, at the Institute for Astronomy at University of Sydney (Australia), researches and writes about fine tuning. His Cambridge University Press book on the subject is due out by the end of 2016. A good place to start in the peer-reviewed literature would be Dr. Barnes' article, which serves as a literature review: Dr. Luke Barnes, The Fine-Tuning of the Universe for Intelligent Life, *Publications of the Astronomical Society of Australia*, 29 (2012) 529. An expanded (77 page) version of this article can be read (free of charge) in Cornell University's online library. The 196 books and

articles he references should keep passionate researchers busy for a while.

Exhibit 7
The Order and Laws of our Universe

Albert Einstein (1879-1955)

When Albert Einstein was asked in an interview if he believed in God, he responded:

> "I'm not an atheist. The problem involved is too vast for our limited minds. We are in the position of a little child entering a huge library filled with books in many languages. The child knows someone must have written those books. It does not know how. It does not understand the languages in which they are written. The child dimly suspects a mysterious order in the arrangement of the books but doesn't know what it is. That, it seems to me, is the attitude of even the most intelligent human being toward God. We see the universe marvelously arranged and obeying certain laws but only dimly understand these laws."[1]

Einstein's scientific hero was Isaac Newton, whose picture was prominently displayed in Einstein's office. Newton wrote, in his famous *Philosophiæ Naturalis Principia Mathematica* (one of the most influential scientific works of all time),

> "This most beautiful system of sun, planets and comets could only proceed from the counsel and domination of an intelligent and powerful Being."[2]

Isaac Newton (1642-1727)
Statue Displayed at Oxford University

I've never traced this story down to confirm its veracity, but even if it's apocryphal, it provides a good illustration of this line of argument. A skeptic supposedly visited Newton in his office and was mesmerized by his model of the solar system. The conversation went something like this:

"Who made your model?" asked the skeptic.

Newton replied, "Nobody."

"Of course somebody made it, and he was brilliant," replied the skeptic.

Newton replied, "If this small model of the universe can't be explained without a creator, how much less can we explain the real solar system and its accompanying laws without a Creator?"

Not convincing at all - 0 1 2 3 4 5 6 7 8 9 10 - Totally Convincing

For Further Seeking

In the following interview, cosmologist Alexander Vilenkin argues that the universe could have begun out of nothing (no time, no space, no matter), because of the bizarre nature of the laws of quantum physics. But note the end of the interview. This would require there to be something prior to the Big Bang—the quantum laws of physics. So where did the laws come from? He admits that this is a mystery.

http://now.tufts.edu/articles/beginning-was-beginning

Newton and Einstein conclude that a higher Intelligence must be responsible for such laws. On Einstein's belief in God, see Walter Isaacson, *Einstein*, pp. 384-393. David Berlinski's *Newton's Gift* gives an insightful look at Newton. See especially pp. 170-174, regarding this line of argument.

Exhibit 8
The Vast Complexity of the Earliest Cells
The Origin of Life

Biological evolution can't explain the origin of cells, since living cells must first exist to allow for the processes of evolution, such as mutations and survival of the fittest. So how do we explain the random, apparently chance appearance of living cells, which we now know to be mind-bogglingly complex? They appear to be the very antithesis of our experience with the productive powers of random chance and more consistent with our experience of design by a personal agent or agents.

Eminent astrophysicist and mathematician Sir Fred Hoyle adopted atheism early in life, only to be pulled in during his mature years, seemingly kicking and screaming, to acknowledge a Grand Designer. His reason? He took the time to meticulously calculate the mathematical odds of the earliest cells being formed by chance, laying out his mathematical reasoning in his book, *The Mathematics of Evolution,* and ruminating on the implications in *Evolution from Space.*[1]

The odds he calculated of a functional protein or enzyme (parts of cells) forming by chance were astronomical: one chance in $10^{40,000}$, which is essentially indistinct from zilch. (To put this huge number in perspective, there are only 10^{80} atoms in the entire universe.)

Another way to put it: Take all the atoms in the universe. Put a mark on one of them and shuffle them thoroughly. Your chance of reaching out with microscopic tweezers and randomly grabbing the marked atom are 1 chance in 10^{80}. But Hoyle's odds are unimaginably smaller than that. And Hoyle isn't a lone outlier with his dismal assessment of the odds.[2]

Hoyle concluded,

> "The notion that not only the biopolymer but the operating program of a living cell could be arrived at by chance in a primordial organic soup here on the Earth is evidently nonsense of a high order."

To illustrate this high improbably, Hoyle rolled out a couple of analogies.

First he compared the chance of getting a single functioning protein from randomly combining amino acids to a solar system full of blind men solving their Rubik's Cubes simultaneously.[3]

Secondly, he compared the odds of the simplest cell forming by chance to the likelihood that "a tornado sweeping through a junkyard might assemble a Boeing 747" passenger jet.

To make the outlandish odds work, without invoking intelligent design, Hoyle suggested that since the age of the earth didn't allow for enough time, much of the random combining must have happened in space, before crashing to the earth. And since the Big Bang theory severely limited the time span of the universe, he argued for a steady state theory (eternal universe) over and against the Big Bang.

But eventually, he reluctantly concluded that even given development in space and a steady state universe, the odds suggest that "a super intellect has monkeyed with the physics, as well as with chemistry and biology, and...there are no blind forces worth speaking about in nature."[4]

Counter Argument

In *The God Delusion*, Richard Dawkins cites Hoyle's Boeing 747 analogy, but argues that we can overcome those seemingly impossible odds once we understand how to work with large numbers.[5] The solution to Hoyle's troubling odds, according to Dawkins, is "statistically informed science."[6]

Here's how it works:

Let's say that we have a billion billion planets in our universe. Let's further imagine that a billion of those planets could sustain life. So if the odds of a cell coming together by chance were one in a billion, then the odds favor a living cell developing on one of those planets. Since we're here to talk about it, we obviously live on the lucky planet. Statistical problem solved!

Reply

But did Dawkins solve Hoyle's problem? That sounds too easy. I mean, Hoyle was a pretty smart guy, so why didn't he think of that in his years of ruminating and three books on the subject?

My first observation is that Dawkins switched numbers on us. (Hoyle had died a few years before Dawkins wrote his book. It would have been interesting to hear Hoyle's reply.) Hoyle actually took the time to calculate and publish his odds back in 1981 for all to see and critique. Again, his odds were one chance in $10^{40,000}$, a number that I find often cited today in discussions of this topic. Surely Dawkins was aware of it.

Yet Dawkins seemingly pulls his own one in a billion odds (one chance in 10^9) out of his hat, a number which conveniently makes for good odds when compared to his estimate of suitable planets. But notice: Dawkins' number provides unimaginably better odds than Hoyle calculated.

So where did Dawkins get his one in a billion estimate? Did he ever take the time to calculate the odds, as Hoyle did? Did he take his odds from some consensus of astrophysicist mathematicians? He gives no justification in either the text or endnotes, yet he claims that his one in a billion works for "even the most pessimistic estimate of the probability that life might spontaneously originate."[7]

So even if Dawkins deemed Hoyle's estimate as way overboard, wouldn't Hoyle's odds at least qualify for "the most pessimistic" category? Rather than examining

Hoyle's math, Dawkins completely ignores it and seems to have created a convenient number out of thin air, claiming that "statistically informed science" solved the problem.

Now I'm no mathematician, and I'm no astrophysicist; but then again, neither is Dawkins. He's a scientist and a good writer, but his specialty is animal behavior[8], not astrophysics, and he admits in his autobiography that math isn't his forte.[9]

Statue of Fred Hoyle (1915-2001)
Outside of the Institute of Astronomy, Cambridge University

Hoyle, by contrast, won the prestigious Mayhew prize (honoring those who distinguish themselves in math and statistics) during his time at Cambridge. He would later teach at Cambridge, leading their Institute of Theoretical Astronomy, being knighted for his unique contributions to the field. So for Dawkins to suggest that the problem with Hoyle's argument is that those who believe it have a hard time comprehending big numbers is quite a stretch. I suspect that most astrophysicists have conjured up at least two thoughts involving numbers in the billions before eating breakfast.

A Related Momentous Event in Philosophy

Moving from science to philosophy, it should be noted that in 2004, Antony Flew, one of the most influential atheist philosophers of the 1900s, announced that he now believed in God. According to Flew, he changed his mind

> "almost entirely because of the DNA investigations. What I think the DNA material has done is that it has shown, by the almost unbelievable complexity of the arrangements which are needed to produce (life), that intelligence must have been involved in getting these extraordinarily diverse elements to work together. It's the enormous complexity of the number of elements and the enormous subtlety of the ways they work

together. The meeting of these two parts at the right time by chance is simply minute. It is all a matter of the enormous complexity by which the results were achieved, which looked to me like the work of intelligence."[10]

Extraordinary Claims

Some have said that extraordinary claims demand extraordinary evidence. Often, they invoke this statement to declare that they could never have enough evidence to believe in something as extraordinary as a personal God. But surely what we deem extraordinary is heavily dependent upon our existing worldviews. What's extraordinary to one person might be quite ordinary to another.

In the case of the origin of life, both Hoyle and Flew think it's quite extraordinary to claim that the simplest cells, which are exceedingly complex, could have come into existence by chance through purely naturalistic means. Surely such an extraordinary claim would demand extraordinary evidence. So just what is the extraordinary evidence that it happened naturalistically?

The evidence offered by Dawkins in chapter four of *The God Delusion* is twofold. First he switches the numbers to make them coincide with his guess as to the number of habitable planets (although we've yet to discover even one habitable planet). Second, he suggests that since evolution showed us how simple life can transform naturalistically over time into complex life, we should all hope that one day someone will suggest a workable way for nonlife to overcome the odds of transforming into life.[11]

The "evidence" Dawkins has proposed seems more like a hunch or a wish (odds with no justification) than legitimate evidence. So where's the extraordinary evidence to support his extraordinary claim?

So to you, which hypothesis—naturalism or supernaturalism—best accounts for the emergence of living cells?

Not convincing at all - 0 1 2 3 4 5 6 7 8 9 10 - Totally Convincing

For Further Seeking

Hoyle's *Mathematics of Evolution* requires some mathematical expertise, yet anyone can skip around and profit from his conclusions at each point. Hoyle and his Cambridge cohort N.C. Wickramasinghe combined their considerable bandwidth to produce *Evolution from Space*. Their writing can actually be pretty creative and fun. Especially note the Introduction, Chapter 9 ("Convergence to God") and Conclusion, for the topic of this section. I should probably also read Hoyle's 1984 work, *The Intelligent Universe,* which presumably sums up those earlier two books and adds further reflections. Another great writer, from the perspective of a microbiologist, is Michael Denton, in his influential *Evolution: A Theory in Crisis*. Denton deals with the origin of life, but looks further for bewildering complexity in more advanced creatures. Denton is a fine researcher as well as wordsmith. For those with patience for detail, Stephen Meyer's recent (2009) *Signature in the Cell* (600+ pages), is a treasure trove of research, organization, and incisive reasoning. Philosopher Antony Flew writes about his own conversion from atheism, primarily because of the DNA evidence, in his book, *There Is a God*.

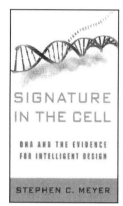

Exhibit 9
The Complexity of Living Creatures

Professor of biochemistry (Lehigh University) Michael Behe is quick to separate himself from young earth creationists. He believes in evolution. He believes the universe is billions of years old. He believes that all organisms share a common ancestor.[1]

But Behe holds that purely naturalistic Darwinian forces can't adequately explain many of the features of living cells or creatures, such as Celia or Flagella or blood clotting or a cell's delivery system. Such features appear to be "irreducibly complex," such that feature "A" couldn't have developed without feature "B" already in place, yet feature "B" couldn't have developed without feature "A" already in place.

Behe defines irreducible complexity as:

> "A single system which is composed of several interacting parts that contribute to the basic function, and where the removal of any one of the parts causes the system to effectively cease functioning."[2]

The Bacterium Flagellum

A flagellum is a microscopic, molecular "motor" that allows bacteria (single cell organisms) to swim. Think of an outboard motor on a boat. Remove the gas tank or spark plug and it won't work at all. It needs all its parts to function. The same goes for the parts comprising the flagellum. To function properly, its 40 plus unique protein parts must be in place and seamlessly interact.

Readers actually need to see a visual representation of a flagellum to understand its complexity and how the parts interact, showing its similarities to an outboard motor. (I had difficulty securing permission to replicate an appropriate graphic, so I'll link you to one embedded in an online article. If you're interested in this line of argument, you'll want to reflect upon the graphic I link to below, or search "bacterium flagellum" in Google, then click "Images" in the search area, to find many representations.)

http://www.evolutionnews.org/2011/03/michael_behe_hasnt_been_refute044801.html

Behe argues that this biological motor is irreducibly complex. For it to function at all, each and every part must be in place at once. Let's imagine that far back in time, before a flagellum existed, that by chance, an outer membrane, cytoplasmic membrane and M ring somehow came together. Of what possible use would this random collection of parts serve? Of what use is a rotor without the S ring and M ring to allow it to rotate? Why would it survive over the years while the rest of the motor was randomly being assembled? How could a flagellum have formed in this way naturalistically, by minute changes and additions, over vast periods of time?[3]

Counter Argument

Richard Dawkins counters that Roman arches appear to be impossible to construct, but they're constructed by building a scaffold to support the arch until the arch is completed, after which the scaffolding is removed. Similarly, suggests Dawkins, complex biological systems may have developed in such a way that eliminated transitional structures that are no longer needed. Thus, current systems may merely *appear* to be irreducibly complex in their present state.[4]

[Note that the former line of argument (Exhibit 8) dealt solely with the origin of the first living cells: the original enzymes, proteins, and cells. The present argument goes beyond cells to include the development of complex biological structures in highly developed living creatures.]

Reply

I'm afraid that, not being a biologist, I'm incompetent to argue in depth on such matters, since biologists argue back and forth (often with remarkable bravado and emotion and name calling) and eventually make claims and counter claims that only biologists can presumably unravel. So although I've read a good bit on this issue, I'll have to remain a bit agnostic in my personal conclusion. But from my present state of understanding as a non-specialist, naturalistic explanations still seem to be quite a stretch.

I *will* say that Michael Denton's book, *Evolution: A Theory in Crisis*, has influenced my thinking. It was a very well researched, well-written, compelling read. It, however, goes way beyond the specific issue of irreducible complexity. Denton's book leads me to believe that it's unlikely that the currently understood mechanisms of evolution (particularly as presented in the simplistic forms promoted by Dawkins and Daniel Dennett), can sufficiently explain many unique features, such as the transition from non-winged creatures to winged creatures (Denton, at one juncture, waxes eloquently on the complexity of feathers), whether or not they're *irreducibly* complex.

In brief, according to classic Darwinism, to evolve from a non-winged creature to a winged creature would require an enormous amount of minute steps over an enormous amount of time. Yet, very few of these steps would seem to provide a distinct survival advantage. In fact, until everything was sufficiently in place (minutely interconnected feathers, hollow bones for lightness, etc.) the poor creature would be stuck with "under construction wings" that would surely be a *disadvantage* to survival at many stages. Thus, many would argue that some kind of pre-programming, with an end purpose in mind, must have been embedded to move a creature toward such a design.[5]

It's surely of great psychological and sociological interest that some people study evolution and come away convinced that the classic mechanisms (e.g., mutations and survival of the fittest) are adequate to explain all the complexities of nature, while others study evolution and come away convinced that the suggested mechanisms come up short. Charles Darwin, interestingly enough, in his final edition of *Origin of the Species*, put himself in the latter category. As he put it:

> "I am convinced that natural selection has been the main but not the exclusive means of modification."[6]

In light of this, perhaps he would have more in common with writers like Denton than we first imagine. At the very least, we should be allowed to ask these questions and formulate our own opinions.

Do you think it's more likely that complex structures developed due to a Designer than to purely naturalistic processes?

Not convincing at all - 0 1 2 3 4 5 6 7 8 9 10 - Totally Convincing

For Those Who Want to Seek Further

For more on irreducible complexity, read Michael Behe's *Darwin's Black Box.* The specific issue of the bacterium flagellum has been debated back and forth, seemingly *ad infinitum*, but here's a blog post to plunge you into the fray: http://www.evolutionnews.org/2011/03/michael_behe_hasnt_been_refute0448 01.html Look beyond irreducible complexity with *Evolution: A Theory in Crisis*, by Michael Denton. Next I'd read Richard Dawkins, *The Blind Watchmaker*, to see how a traditional evolutionist would respond to some of Behe's and Denton's arguments. Be aware, however, that Harvard's Stephen Jay Gould, highly regarded as one of modern times' most revered experts on evolution, strongly disagreed with some of Dawkins' teachings on evolution, deriding him as a "fundamentalist." To see Gould's critique, begin with this review in *The New York Review of Books* http://www.nybooks.com/articles/1997/06/12/darwinian-fundamentalism/ and find part two here: http://www.nybooks.com/articles/1997/06/26/evolution-the-pleasures-of-pluralism/ .

Section 3
Existential Fit

Exhibit 10

Belief in God Seems to "Fit" Life as We Experience It, Making Life Better

A part of truth-seeking can be: "Try it and see if it works."

Example: I was prescribed high-dose Niacin to boost my good cholesterol. The listed possible side effects seemed innocuous and transitory, such as "a mild flushing." So I tried it. "Mild flushing," in my case, turned my face red as a beet, and set my body on fire. After it happened several times, I concluded, "This can't be good for me!" My personal experience with high dose Niacin taught me something that the initial scientific studies apparently failed to reveal: "flushing" can be wicked and some people simply can't tolerate it.

We learn much through personal experience and the experiences of others. Buddhism recommends that people seek truth, in part, by trying a recommended path to personally test its usefulness. The Hebrew Psalmist urged people to "Taste and see that the LORD is good."[1] Philosophers C. S. Peirce and

William James defined and defended a nuanced form of "Pragmatism" to test truth claims, an approach which became quite influential.

Applying this pragmatic approach to our choice between worldviews, surely it's valuable to see how they work out in real life. After all, the Psalmist states that the person who follows a godly path is "blessed," or "happy."[2] Jesus said that He came to give life in abundance.[3] Those would seem to be testable claims. Does following God make life better?

Objection

"I could collect testimonies of people who claim that heroin changed their lives for the better. Making life better doesn't necessarily make one path truer than another."

Response

Agreed. But heroin provides short-term ecstasy, at the price of long-term misery. Here we're looking for a philosophy of life that brings a longer, richer fulfillment, close to the Hebrew term "blessed." Now granted, there's no airtight logical formula stating that what makes us happier is true; but surely, when we're choosing a life course, that which works to give a fuller life should be considered, even if it merely takes a worldview from being summarily dismissed to being plausible.

But beyond providing live options, could higher levels of satisfaction with life point to something significant about life's origin, purpose and meaning? After all, perhaps we were created to live this way, so that the resulting fulfillment resonates with people, indicating they made a sound choice.

Studies on Life Satisfaction and Happiness

Once upon a time, Psychologists primarily studied miserable people to discover what made them miserable. Then, in the 1980s and 1990s, psychologists made a concerted effort to study happy people to discover what makes them happy. The results were interesting.

When psychologist David Myers surveyed the literature on happiness, he found that "Survey after survey across North America and Europe reveals that religious people more often than nonreligious people report feeling happy and satisfied with life."[4] A Gallup survey compared those low in spiritual commitment with those high in spiritual commitment and found that "The highly spiritual were twice as likely to say they were "very happy."[5]

But *Why* Are They Happier?

I'm not sure. Some say that God simply infused them with joy. Alternatively, perhaps the behaviors emphasized by their religion make for happiness. Psychologists can list habits and qualities that result in greater happiness. These include happiness-producing behaviors such as giving, forgiving, prioritizing relationships, being thankful, being less selfish, not being materialistic, etc.

By contrast, when prominent philosopher Alex Rosenberg tries to lay out in detail the implications of his atheistic worldview, it seems rather depressing. There's no free will, no right and wrong, no ultimate purpose in life, no ultimate meaning, no values that really matter, no inherent rights (clumps of matter don't have rights). Nothing we do will really matter in the long haul, according to Rosenberg, since there's no life after death and the universe is doomed to die a cold death. If that depresses you, Rosenberg suggests taking Prozac.[6]

The problem is that it's difficult, if not impossible, to live consistently with Rosenberg's worldview as he lays it out. It's that pragmatism thing. As someone observed in reviewing Rosenberg's book, the world that he describes is not the world we live in. In the world as we experience it, we strongly sense right and wrong, meaningful decisions, purpose, values, and the innate worth of human beings.[7] And those are often closely tied with experiencing happiness.

So How Is This Evidence for God?

Perhaps it goes back to looking at the world as we experience it and seeing which worldview fits better with the data—a theistic worldview or an atheistic worldview. If we indeed live in a world where we strongly sense that people are more than robots—our decisions matter, a human life is of great worth, certain practices are just plain right or wrong—then we may decide that Rosenberg's worldview must somehow be flawed.

Surely even Rosenberg can't live consistently with his view. And no matter what Rosenberg declares about right and wrong being subjective, if a woman he loves cheats on him, or if someone wrongfully fires him from his job, surely something wells up inside him and he declares, "You were wrong!" And no matter how much he says that we can't make a difference, he sure writes like he thinks he's making a difference in what people think.

What can you learn from your own life experience, regarding right and wrong, decision making, human rights, etc.? Which worldview best explains life as you've experienced it?

Myriads of people testify that they had gone astray in life; but once they connected with God, they "found meaning," "discovered fullness of life," "found a reason to live," "got new direction," "figured out why I was here," "found the joy I'd been missing." As C. S. Lewis put it, he was "surprised by joy."[8]

So for many, this "fit with life" or "now it all makes sense" is a pointer to something larger, an indication that they've found what life was meant to be.

Now all this sounds very touchy-feely, and perhaps it is, but surely emotional intelligence helps us to understand life. While I gravitate toward analytical phrases such as "logically follows," or "has sufficient evidence," those who get the present line of argument use phrases like "resonates with me" or "just feels right." And while such approaches to truth can lead people astray, surely they can also be an important part of understanding life.

A man lacking emotional intelligence may call his wife a week before Christmas and say,

> "Honey, do you remember back when we first got married and we were barely making ends meet? We were in that jewelry store and we saw that beautiful ring and I said, 'One day we'll have some money and I'll buy that for you?'"
>
> (Pause…)
>
> "Well, I'm in the gun shop next door to that shop. Can you meet me here with the debit card? I need to pick up some ammo."

After he hangs up, he can't imagine why his wife got angry. My point? There are some truths about how life works that are better grasped through emotional intelligence than strictly logical intelligence.[9]

I'm still not satisfied with the line of argument here. Yet, it seems to be strongly compelling to many. Perhaps it's just something you've got to "taste and see."

Not convincing at all - 0 1 2 3 4 5 6 7 8 9 10 – Totally Convincing

For Those Who Want to Seek Further

David Myers is a respected psychologist, who has written numerous psychology textbooks, as well as books exploring spirituality. Two of his books relevant to this chapter include *The Pursuit of Happiness* and *The American Paradox.* I suppose the largest and most recent study of youth and spirituality is the *National Study on Youth and Religion* (http://youthandreligion.nd.edu/). It is a longitudinal study, but the first work I read on the preliminary results was *Soul Searching: The Religious and Spiritual Lives of American Teenagers*, by Christian Smith with Melinda Lundquist Denton (New York: Oxford University Press, 2005.) See especially chapter 7: "Adolescent Religion and Life Outcomes," which found spiritually committed teens experienced less guilt, more happiness, etc., than their uncommitted peers.

Exhibit 11

Many Attest to Sensing a God-shaped Vacuum That Could Only Be Filled with God

Augustine of Hippo (354-430)
17th Century Portrait by Philippe de Champaigne

Augustine grew up as a deep thinker and wisdom-seeker with a sex-charged wild side. His journey to peace with God, chronicled in his famous *Confessions*, included a philosophical journey (from Manichaeism to Platonism) and a mystical experience (hearing a voice telling him to read a portion of the Bible). But he also reflected upon a heart element. In his own words, expressed as a prayer,

"You have made us for yourself, O Lord, and our hearts are restless until they rest in you."[1]

Others have expressed some missing piece that God filled. Scientist Blaise Pascal put it this way:

> "What else does this craving, and this helplessness, proclaim but that there was once in man a true happiness, of which all that now remains is the empty print and trace? This he tries in vain to fill with everything around him, seeking in things that are not there the help he cannot find in those that are, though none can help, since this infinite abyss can be filled only with an infinite and immutable object; in other words by God himself."[2]

Perhaps these experiences were similar to what C. S. Lewis described:

> "If I find in myself a desire which no experience in this world can satisfy, the most probable explanation is that I was made for another world."[3]

Could this also be the feeling associated with what many people call the "witness of the Spirit," which philosopher William Craig cites as a primary reason to acknowledge God?[4]

Ruminations on Such Experiences

Now I have to admit that I tend to look skeptically at such "feelings" and "heart matters." Perhaps I'm not in touch enough with my feelings, but I see many people putting *too much* trust in their feelings to make big decisions and later regretting them. Some friends "just knew" that their emotional obsession of the month was "Miss Right." Others "just knew" the entrepreneurial decision was right. But often acting on "just knowing" resulted in poor decisions.

But while I tend to look skeptically at my feelings, surely I shouldn't discount them altogether. Why would I marry someone if the objective data (compatibility, etc.) added up, but I "just felt in my heart that it was wrong?"

My wide reading in biography also shows me the intellectual impact of filling this inner void.

- Bertrand Russell, the famous atheist philosopher of the 1900s, had a daughter who studied at some top universities and exhibited a first-rate intellect. But after getting married, she felt strongly that something was missing in her life and suggested to her husband that they attend church. Over time, that emptiness was filled to the extent that they embarked upon mission work in Africa.[5]

- When popular author Anne Rice (Think: *Interview with a Vampire*) began to move as a mature adult from atheism to theism, her reasons seemed more emotional than purely rational. Even before she answered her intellectual questions, she felt in her heart that God was pursuing her and there were indeed answers out there.[6]

Many intelligent people allow their hearts to impact their religious decisions. Perhaps Pascal was onto something when he wrote,

"The heart has its reasons of which reason knows nothing."[7]

An Illustration

Imagine that, just this moment, you found yourself in a garden spot, with no other humans in sight, with no memories of a personal past. As you explore the garden and observe the sky, you begin to experience a new feeling in your stomach. You don't know what it means, but instinctively feel a need to put something in your mouth and chew. You try a leaf, but it tastes bitter and does nothing to quell the curious empty feeling. Eventually you feel physically weak. Then you notice the red apples hanging from the tree. You eat one. It tastes good, satisfies the empty feeling, and your energy returns.

You conclude that you've discovered something important about yourself. Eating food satisfies that empty feeling in your stomach. Although you have no understanding of the underlying biological mechanisms, you intuit the bigger picture. "Perhaps I'm onto something," you reason. "Perhaps eating is important to staying healthy, even my physical survival. From now on, when I feel hungry, I'll eat."

Later that evening, you observe another feeling, this one less physical and more emotional—a psychological longing. As you observe the leaves more closely, they appear to be very intricate, with a sort of skeletal system to keep them from flopping, containing apparently some kind of feeding system related to the tree. Those observations cause you to reflect on the power of your eyes to see both far and near, to distinguish shapes and colors. "Wow!" you think. "These eyes and leaves are spectacular!" Then you extend your thought to the animals and plants and stars in the sky. You conclude, "Whoever designed these must have been extremely smart and talented."

Since you don't see such a designer, you instinctually bow your head and breathe a word of praise and thanks to whoever made leaves, eyes, animals and stars. Immediately, the psychological emptiness seems to have been filled.

You reflect upon this psychological experience. Just as eating food filled a physical need, so the humble acknowledgement and praise of "Whoever Made This Stuff" filled a psychological need. "Perhaps I'm onto something," you reason. "Perhaps just as there are needs of the body, there are other needs— needs of the heart—that are filled when I acknowledge and praise Whoever is behind all I see."

Assessment

Again, as with the last line of evidence, I'm not satisfied with this as an empirically and logically tight argument. Surely many naturalistic explanations for such felt needs and such satisfactions of needs can be forwarded. But somehow it's very persuasive to many. Perhaps for many it's just one piece of the puzzle that helps complete the picture provided by other lines of evidence.

Not convincing at all - 0 1 2 3 4 5 6 7 8 9 10 - Totally Convincing

Suggested Reading

Peter Kreef, professor of philosophy at Boston College, runs this line of argument here: http://www.peterkreeft.com/topics/desire.html . C. S. Lewis argues from innate desires to the existence of God in *Mere Christianity*, Book III, chapter 10. For Lewis' ruminations on joy, see *Surprised by Joy*. Here are a few modern biographies that speak to me on this subject: Katherine Tait, *My Father, Bertrand Russell*, and Peter Hitchens, *The Rage Against God*. In each case, they speak more in terms of "The Hound of Heaven" pursuing them, than being won over by some purely intellectual line of reasoning.[8]

Exhibit 12
Often a Paradigm Shift or Gestalt Experience
Leads to a New View of Reality

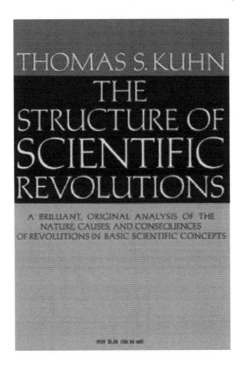

A Scientist Sees Design

About 30 years ago I heard a scientist speak at Dalton State University on his sudden change from atheist/agnostic to believer. As I recall, he taught at the University of Chicago. He spoke of formerly holding the view that the universe was sufficiently explained as being the product of natural causes. Then, one night as he was looking at the sky, he suddenly saw design and purpose behind it all. It was the same sky as he'd always seen and studied. But suddenly, he saw the same data through a different "set of glasses" and it made better sense to him through the new glasses.

The Priority of the Paradigm

Thomas Kuhn, in his influential book *The Structure of Scientific Revolutions*, gives example after example of how difficult it is for scientists to break out of their old scientific paradigms to adopt new scientific theories. Even when the evidence accumulates that the old paradigm is defunct, there's a strong tendency to hold for dear life onto the old paradigm and keep propping it up with more and more complex rationalizations.[1]

The Gestalt Experience

Sometimes, even for scientists, it's not "a bit more evidence" that's needed to make the shift to a new theory, but something akin to a gestalt moment, much like the above scientist experienced, where his mind simply shifted from one perspective to another, seeing the same data through a different set of eyes.

As a graphic example, what do you see here?

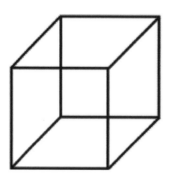 

Is the left side of the box in the front, or the back? Is the image on the right a goblet or two faces? Although the image (our data) doesn't change, our way of viewing it does change.

Peter Hitchens Has a Religious Paradigm Shift

Peter Hitchens burnt his Bible in high school and experienced great freedom in being able to do whatever he wanted to do. Like many in 1960s England, he also burnt his parents' morals, and his elders' political outlook (what he called the "Churchhill Cult").

Later in life, as a successful, well-paid journalist, he covered stories from a beautiful section of London, with plenty of money to vacation with his girlfriend on holidays. Everyone he knew shared his worldview (his girlfriend was raised a Marxist atheist), and if he discovered an acquaintance who believed in God, he reacted with shock and something akin to a physical revulsion. According to Hitchens, "My life was devoted largely to pleasure and ambition."

But in his 30s, great architecture and paintings and music began to "speak" to him. He loved Philip Larkin's line:

> "The trees are coming into leaf,
>   like something almost being said."

What did architecture "say" to him?

The great medieval churches reminded him that he would one day die. The elaborate architecture reminded him that the builders couldn't have been morons. They were highly skilled, and often claimed that their skill was enhanced or motivated by their faith. Those observations softened his arrogance toward older generations and their ways.

One day in his early 30s, on holiday with his girlfriend, in search of fine food and wine, he saw a painting that rocked his comfortable paradigm. It was Rogier van der Weyden's fifteenth century painting, *The Last Judgment*. Somehow, it "spoke" to him...powerfully. According to Hitchens, it wasn't a mystical experience,

> "But I had a sudden, strong sense of religion being a thing of the present day, not imprisoned under thick layers of time."

For Hitchens, this paradigm shift jolted him back to God—a shift to a new way of looking at things that has remained with him for 30 years.[2] It's interesting that Hitchens reflected that if it were possible to reach his brother, the famous atheist Christopher Hitchens, it would most likely be by "the unexpected force of poetry, which can ambush the heart at any time."[3]

Does it make sense that, in many cases, it takes a paradigm shift, rather than just new evidence, to open eyes to God?

Not convincing at all - 0 1 2 3 4 5 6 7 8 9 10 - Totally Convincing

Suggested Reading

Again, I tend to value arguments that are more evidential and analytical. So I was a bit disappointed in my first reading of Hitchens to find him not immersing himself in evidential literature. But after a second look, his conversion helped me to see that for many people, it's not a problem of insufficient or erroneous data. In their cases, they simply needed something to jolt them out of their old way of viewing the data, to see the same data through different eyes. For that reason, read Peter Hitchens' *The Rage Against God: How Atheism Led Me to Faith,* and see how his journey strikes you. Perhaps Anne Rice's *Called Out of Darkness* is another such story.[4]

Exhibit 13
Such Vivid Experiences as Consciousness and Free Will
Seem to be Better Explained by the Existence of Nonmaterial
Minds/Souls That are Separate from the Brain

In reading atheist Susan Blackmore's book, *Dying to Live*, in which she tried to explain near-death experiences in naturalistic terms, I fully expected her to explain away the "realer than real" experience of NDErs with something like, "Hey, just because something *seems* real doesn't mean that it *is* real." Instead, she led readers down a far different path.

She claimed that according to naturalistic, reductionist science, consciousness and decision-making are both illusions. There's no "I" in a command center, in which we sit over our brains to direct our thinking.[1]

Since our brains are analogous to advanced computers, think of it this way. It's silly to think of computers making decisions of their own free will. They merely do what they're programmed to do. In the same way, according to Blackmore, our brains have been programmed through natural selection to think in a certain way. Thus, everything our brains think is what they've been "programmed" to think.

Thus, there is no free will, no "I" choosing what to think about. Even consciousness is an illusion.

And Blackmore isn't some odd person out in this assessment. Atheist Philosopher Alex Rosenberg, in his recent *The Atheist's Guide to Reality*, argues similarly. He goes so far as to say that anyone who builds his worldview exclusively on science ("scientism") must agree that there is no "I". Such vivid experiences as consciousness and free will are simply illusions.[2]

Now I don't want to imply that all atheists hold to Rosenberg's and Blackmore's views on such matters. But for those who do, I'd suggest that they can't live consistently with such views. After they declare that "I" doesn't exist, they keep right on referring to "I," "me," and "we." If none of "us" exist, then who, may I ask, are they referring to? And since Blackmore's and Rosenberg's brains apparently go about their business without any interference from a directing mind, then how do they propose to influence other brains? If they truly believe that brains think only what they're programmed to think, then how can they be so sure that their views on anything are correct; and why are they writing books to try to persuade other minds to presumably "choose" their views over other views?

The outcome is that their views don't seem to jive with the reality that we directly experience, very vividly, every waking moment. What we *do* experience is consistent with the idea that we *are* able to choose much of what we think and we *do* have minds that make real decisions, even if we can't remove a mind and physically examine it in a laboratory.

The view that we do indeed have minds separate from our brains fits well into a supernatural worldview that acknowledges minds. To me, it doesn't seem to fit well into a naturalistic worldview, at least the one as described by Blackmore and Rosenberg.

Not convincing at all - 0 1 2 3 4 5 6 7 8 9 10 - Totally Convincing

Suggested Reading

For Alex Rosenberg's arguments, see his *Atheist's Guide to Reality*. For Susan Blackmore's argument, see her *Dying to Live*, toward the end of chapter 7. To see a brief, current defense of the mind, see Thomas Nagel's review of John Searle's *The Rediscovery of the Mind*, http://www.nybooks.com/articles/1993/03/04/the-mind-wins/.

I've not read enough on this subject, except in regards to how near-death experiences give evidence of both a mind separate from the brain, as well as the spiritual context (a supernatural realm) in which this occurs. You might also read, *Where the Conflict Really Lies*, by Alvin Plantinga, where he seeks to demonstrate that our experience of rationality fits better with a theistic rather than naturalistic worldview.

J.P. Moreland is a distinguished professor of philosophy (with a background in chemistry as well) who has written extensively concerning philosophy of mind.

For all issues touching on philosophy (such as the mind/body problem) consult the free, peer-reviewed, online *Stanford Encyclopedia of Philosophy* for an authoritative, balanced overview and starting point.

Exhibit 14

Such Vivid Experiences as Objective Morals
Are Best Explained by an Objective Law–Giver

Statue of Immanuel Kant (1724-1804) in Kaliningrad, Russia

A Pretty Deep Thinker

Immanuel Kant was one of the most influential philosophers of all time. As such, he's typically toward the top of people's lists of brainy people.

(**Tip**: Want to be considered a deep thinker? Backpack a copy of Kant's *Critique of Pure Reason* and pretend to be reading it whenever attempting to impress someone.)

It's intriguing that such a deep thinker should narrow down two things that especially arrested his thought:

"Two things fill the mind with ever new and increasing admiration and awe, the more often and steadily we reflect upon them: the starry heavens above me and the moral law within me."[1]

Out of all Kant's writings, his friends chose that sentence for the inscription on his tombstone.

In college, when I first read C.S. Lewis' rendition of the moral argument, I gave it little credence. It seemed like rather soft evidence to me–something that could be easily explained away by secular psychology. I gravitated more toward hard data like the beginning of the universe. But realizing that such intellectual heavyweights as Kant and Lewis and Francis Collins take it seriously gives me the nagging feeling that I must have missed something. Indeed, the argument has grown upon me over the years. See what you think.

On Child Torturers, Hitler, and Objective Right and Wrong

So you're carrying on a pleasant conversation with an interesting person at a bus stop, until he admits that he tortures children for fun. You reply in horror, "That's just plain wrong!"

Now think about your response for a minute. Are you merely stating your *subjective* opinion (wrong for me, right for you), or are you stating an *objective* truth (wrong no matter what anyone else thinks)?

I'd suggest that you and I know that it's objectively wrong. You certainly wouldn't respond to the person as if your opinion were merely one *subjective* opinion out of many equally valid opinions. You wouldn't say, "Now torturing innocent children for fun would be wrong for me; but who knows...perhaps it's right for you."

Bottom line: You and I don't believe this is our *subjective* opinion. Rather, we're certain that it's *objective* truth: Torturing innocent children for fun is just plain wrong, no matter what anybody else thinks.

And when we say that some moral truths are objective, we seem to be saying something more. Surely we're saying that there's an objective standard, outside of ourselves (not subjective), that we know we ought to obey.

Naturalism Implies That Right and Wrong are Subjective

But this conclusion seems strangely out of place in a purely naturalistic world. After all, according to naturalism, aren't we nothing more than animals that evolved to be a bit smarter than dolphins and apes? Aren't humans merely, as Richard Dawkins states, hosts for the survival of selfish genes? According to naturalist Alex Rosenberg, there is no objective right or wrong. So who can say (from a naturalistic perspective) that the child torturer, or Hitler for that matter, were *wrong*? At best, we can say that we personally disapprove of what they did.

Within the naturalistic worldview, some would say that survival of the fittest is our primary, if not our sole purpose. We know what that looks like in the animal kingdom, where parent birds sit nonchalantly by as the stronger chicks peck the weaker to death. Yet we don't judge the birds for being immoral any more than we'd judge a robot immoral for torturing a child it was programmed to torture. After all, their actions are determined by their genes and upbringing. How can you blame them? Similarly, under naturalism, why should we blame Hitler?

So it seems that we have two choices. We can either accept naturalism and deny the existence of objective morality, admitting that Hitler's atrocities may be bad for me but good for him, or we can say, "There must be something wrong with naturalism. What Hitler did *was* objectively wrong, and I *know* it!"

But if the naturalistic hypothesis fails to sufficiently explain my moral outrage against Hitler and my vivid experience of objective right and wrong, what worldview might make more sense of it?

Objective Right and Wrong in Theism

A theistic worldview suggests that the reason we believe that both Hitler and child torturers are wrong is that they *are* indeed wrong–objectively wrong. And our vivid experience with right and wrong, which so impressed Kant, and which we can't easily deny, must be rooted in something more objective than the whims of my genes. Thus, many theists suggest that our experience with objective morals makes sense when they're rooted in the character of the God. That explains why we feel bad when we do something wrong and feel moral outrage at Hitler.

Thus, this part of my human experience—my experience with objective right and wrong—seems to make more sense in a theistic worldview than a naturalistic worldview.

Comparing "Better" and "Worse" People Implies an Objective Standard

Bolstering this conclusion is the way we make value judgments. If I say that Nelson Mandela was *better* than Hitler, I must be comparing them both to some objective standard. In a theistic world, the standard could be rooted in the character of God.

By contrast, in a naturalistic world, where would this objective standard "exist?" Surely we'd have to deny that there's any objective standard and have to admit that value judgments are a purely subjective matter, dependent upon which worldviews and personal values we hold.

Let's look a bit further at value judgments through the lens of Richard Dawkins' naturalistic worldview, where our "sole purpose in life" is to pass on the best (most likely to survive) genes to future generations. Through this lens wasn't Hitler at the forefront of trying to move things forward? Perhaps Hitler got it wrong when he decided that entire races were dumber and weaker than others; but had he stuck with eliminating the mentally and physically handicapped (and by necessity all who opposed his agenda), surely he should have been commended for purifying the gene pool and acting in accord with life's purpose.

But most of us can't get away from this strong sense that Hitler was wrong— objectively wrong—and that he was a worse person than Mandela.

Once again, this part of my human experience—my experience with comparing "better and worse" people or "better and worse moral judgments"—seems to make more sense in a theistic worldview than a naturalistic worldview.

Objection

Some argue that, if we root objective right and wrong in the command of God, that we must further ask, "Then is it right because God commands it, or is it right independent of God?" The former reeks of "might means right." The latter fails to answer the question, "where do objective values reside?"

Response

This objection seems to miss the point. Theists tend to argue that it's not the *command* of God that makes something right or wrong, but the *character* of God. In this view, things aren't wrong because God *says* they're wrong, but because they are against His nature, and people were made in His image. That's why we can't get away from right and wrong. That's why we know that objective right and wrong exist. And that's why it makes so much sense that there must be a God behind it all.

William Craig puts this argument in a logical format as follows:

> Premise 1: If God does not exist, objective moral values and duties do not exist.
> Premise 2: Objective moral values and duties do exist.
> Therefore: God exists.

Not convincing at all - 0 1 2 3 4 5 6 7 8 9 10 - Totally Convincing

For Further Searching

Here's a five minute, simple, animated film describing the moral argument: http://www.reasonablefaith.org/moral . Those who want to go deeper can follow the other discussions linked on that same webpage. In my introduction I talked about Francis Collins' journey from atheism to faith. On pages 20-31 of his book, *The Language of God*, he explains the moral argument and how it shook his atheistic foundations. C.S. Lewis describes the moral argument in his classic, *Mere Christianity.*

The online *Stanford Encyclopedia of Philosophy* has a helpful article describing different formulations of this argument, with rebuttals and counter rebuttals, titled Moral Arguments for the Existence of God, with many references to relevant works.

Section 4
The Phenomenon of Widespread Belief
Distinguishes the God Hypothesis
From the Spaghetti Monster Hypothesis

Exhibit 15
Many People, of All Vocations and Levels of Education,
Report a Direct Apprehension of God

Dr. Alvin Plantinga (1932-)
Professor of Philosophy Emeritus (Retired), University of Notre Dame

Some claim to "just know" that God exists. It's not necessarily based on a feeling, or based upon a line of reasoning. They "just know." It's like their belief is a gift from God. Can "just knowing" be a sufficient reason for belief?

Perhaps.

We believe in a physical world outside ourselves because we have such a strong, direct apprehension of it, although we can't prove scientifically that it exists. (Study the history of radical empiricism leading to skepticism). The same goes for our consciousness and free will and belief in other minds and our trust that our reasoning faculties can lead us to higher truths. We can't successfully argue with any finality for the existence or truth of such things. Rather, we just accept them as "basic." In the same way, many people report a direct apprehension of God–an apprehension so strong that they seem to require no additional evidence to believe.

Thus, for them, it's simply not plausible to believe otherwise.

On Plausibility

Imagine Susan Blackmore and Alex Rosenberg arguing with Bart, an intelligent guy on the street, that consciousness is an illusion and that free will doesn't exist. Blackmore and Rosenberg argue that certain experiments and arguments prove their point.

But Bart might well reply incredulously, after hearing their arguments,

> "And you really believe that? I mean, obviously I'm conscious...I'm standing here talking with you. Could there by anything more obvious in the world, both to me and to you, that I'm conscious? In fact, if we're making decisions about what is real by our empirical experience, my own consciousness is one of the most vivid, undeniable experiences that I could possibly have. So whatever your argument is, there's obviously some problem with it. Whatever experiment you're citing, there's obviously something wrong with it. *It's simply not plausible to believe that I'm not a conscious being.*"

This is why a book entitled, *"I'm Conscious...and You're Probably Conscious Too!"* would likely fall stillborn from the press, or sell to only a tiny fringe of philosophers. We *just know* we're conscious. A defense of consciousness would seem hopelessly redundant to most folks. If we can't trust in our own vivid experience of consciousness, why should we trust in the accuracy of our reasoning, much less the reasoning of the philosopher who denies his own consciousness?

Similarly, those who claim to have a strong direct apprehension of God may be disinterested in apologetics, in the same way that those who have travelled around the world probably have very little interest reading a book that sets out to prove that the world is round. Why waste time reading up on "duh" issues?

By contrast, we don't find significant numbers of intelligent, sane people claiming to have an undeniable apprehension of flying spaghetti monsters or fairies, thus distinguishing the God hypothesis from such speculative hypotheses. This is significant sociological data which must be accounted for. It fits with a theistic hypothesis which includes honest seeking eventually leading to faith, since faith might be granted without someone having to be exposed to evidential lines of argument.

Are these "just knowers" more likely deceived (consistent with naturalism), or are they more likely on to something (consistent with theism)? That's the question to consider when deciding which worldview is a better fit.

Not convincing at all – 0 1 2 3 4 5 6 7 8 9 10 - Totally Convincing

To Search Further

A basic summary of this argument is included in Thomas Nagel's (an atheist) review of Alvin Plantinga's (a theist) book, *Where the Conflict Really Lies: Science, Religion and Naturalism* (Oxford University Press). Find the review here: http://www.nybooks.com/articles/2012/09/27/philosopher-defends-religion/ . Those with some philosophical background might consider Plantinga's three-volume magnum opus, *Warrant: The Current Debate*, *Warrant and Proper Function* (both Oxford University Press, 1993) and *Warranted Christian Belief* (Oxford University Press, 2000). Philosopher William Alston argues for the legitimacy of religious experience in his book, *Perceiving God*.

Exhibit 16

Many People, of All Vocations and Levels of Education, Report a Compelling First-Hand Experience with God

Mortimer Adler (1902-2001)

A Philosopher Experiences God

Mortimer Adler, philosopher-at-large, prolific author, and long-time senior editor for *Encyclopedia Britannica*, believed in an impersonal God—not a God one would worship or pray to—from his study of philosophy. It took a compelling first-hand encounter to add personality to his mental picture of God.

After a trip to Mexico, Adler became seriously ill and spent five weeks in a hospital. During that time, a pastor visited him and prayed for his recovery. According to Adler,

> I choked up and wept. The only prayer that I knew word for word, was the *Pater Noster*. On that day and in the days after it, I found myself repeating the Lord's Prayer, again and again, and meaning every word of

it. Quite suddenly, when I was awake one night, a light dawned on me, and I realized what had happened without my recognizing it clearly when first it happened. I had been seriously praying to God....

Reflecting upon that event, Adler wrote:

With no audible voice accessible to me, I was saying voicelessly to myself "Dear God, yes, I do believe, not just in the God my reason so stoutly affirms, but the God to whom Father Howell is now praying, and on whose grace and love I now joyfully rely."

Now some might consider Adler's experience a blind leap of faith. But from his description of the event, he didn't turn off his brilliant mind and make a blind leap to believe in a personal God. Instead, the experience seemed rather passive, like the bridge was crossed from the other side rather than from his side. Rather than *leaping* to belief, he simply *found himself believing*. This might fit well with the "direct apprehension of God" from the last chapter, but it's interesting to see this, in Adler's case, dovetailing with a first-hand, dramatic experience.[1]

An Alcoholic Finds God

Bill Wilson, cofounder of *Alcoholics Anonymous*, was a raging alcoholic who'd tried everything imaginable to get sober. Everything failed, and he considered having himself institutionalized for his own safety and the safety of others. Then a long-time friend and fellow alcoholic, Ebbie Thatcher, showed up at Wilson's house sober. Naturally, Wilson wanted to know the story, but was severely disappointed to hear that Ebbie had gotten religion.

Ebbie recounted the story of a couple of alcoholic friends who travelled to Switzerland to seek help from the famous psychiatrist Carl Jung. Although Jung's efforts failed, he told them that he knew of several alcoholics who'd found sobriety through a religious conversion experience. Ebbie joined the *Oxford Group* in New York–a Christian fellowship made up of almost exclusively intelligent, educated people–where he had his own religious experience and found sobriety. (The principles espoused by this *Oxford Group* were adopted as the famous *Twelve Steps* of *Alcoholics Anonymous*.)

Priding himself on being thoroughly rational and scientific, and feeling that religion was the very antithesis of this, Wilson resisted until he saw no other alternative. Finally, he issued a challenge: "If there be a God, let Him show

Himself now!"

The resulting experience, complete with a room filling with light, an enveloping presence, and a vision of himself on a mountaintop, left him feeling profoundly free. He immediately lost all desire to drink and would never touch alcohol again. After reading similar conversion experiences in William James' (America's most eminent psychologist at the time) *Varieties of Religious Experience*, Wilson felt more settled about his experience.[2]

Naturalists should provide evidence that Wilson's experience is better explained by naturalism than supernaturalism. But note that this was much more than just an "emotional experience," in the sense of a warm, fuzzy feeling. It was empirical and life-changing–something that Wilson saw and experienced–with powerful lingering results (no more drinking), similar to our direct apprehension of a physical world outside of ourselves.

For Wilson, coming from a totally scientific, anti-supernatural bias, this one experience proved to him that God existed. He didn't believe in God by blind faith. Rather, he believed because of what he deemed sufficient evidence.

Not convincing at all – 0 1 2 3 4 5 6 7 8 9 10 - Totally Convincing

For Further Seeking

See Dr. Craig Keener's experience that took him from atheism to theism here: http://www.craigkeener.com/tag/conversion-from-atheism/ (He would eventually write the two volume tome, *Miracles*.) Mortimer Adler recorded his own experience in his book, *A Second Look in the Rearview Mirror*, pp. 276-278. Biographer Francis Hartigan wrote of Bill Wilson's experience in *Bill W.: A Biography of Alcoholics Anonymous Cofounder Bill Wilson*, pp. 56-69. William James' classic *Varieties of Religious Experience* could also be consulted with profit. He believed that evidence for God is primarily found in people's personal experiences, which he studied in great detail in his book. He concluded that "the life of [religion] as a whole is mankind's most important function."[3]

Exhibit 17

Many Respected Intellectuals Believe that Their Line of Reasoning Is Compelling for Belief in God

Dr. Henry Schaefer III (1944-)

Henry Schaefer is one of today's eminent scientists. He has published over 1,000 articles in professional chemistry journals. Out of 628,000 chemists whose work has been cited by others, he's the sixth most cited—57,000 times. His original research involves using computers and theoretical methods to solve problems in molecular quantum mechanics.[1]

He also believes in God—not because of a personal religious experience, or a leap of faith—but because of his systematic and sustained study of the evidence. He grew up in a secular home, but saw the importance of asking ultimate questions, with the God question made a bit more plausible by his encounters with some brilliant, believing scientists he met at M.I.T. and Stanford. Over the years he personally studied many of the issues regarding faith and finally declared himself a believer while he was teaching at Berkeley.

Schaefer's intellectual journey to faith is a well-worn path that has been travelled by many intellectuals throughout history, including eminent historians, archeologists, linguists, philosophers, scientists, psychologists, etc. (See collections of such intellectuals in the recommended reading.)

So What Evidence Does this Provide?

I'm not suggesting that since many smart, informed people, found God through weighing the evidence, that therefore God must exist. That would employ the logical fallacy of believing because of authority. (Similarly, we could present a list of bright people who say they studied the evidence and became atheists.)

I'm merely suggesting that the existence of a large number of brilliant believers should give pause to those who declare dogmatically that faith is necessarily blind. As I mentioned in the introduction, Richard Dawkins stated with an air of finality in an interview that there's "no shred of evidence" for the existence of God. In *The God Delusion* he wrote, "there is no evidence to favor the God Hypothesis."

But surely Henry Schaefer was right to give some evidential weight to his encounters with sincere, brilliant believers at M.I.T. and Stanford. Their very existence suggested to him that they must have some kind of intellectual foundation for their faith. And surely they must have wrestled with the common objections to faith.

There's a reason Schaefer never ran into anyone in academia who believed in a flying spaghetti monster: there's absolutely no evidence for one. The existence of brilliant, informed theists implies that, at least in their minds, there's sufficient evidence to warrant belief. Similarly, the existence of bright agnostics and atheists implies that they have evidence that they believe favors their worldview.

The thoughtful observer of this phenomenon (the coexistence of bright, informed theists and bright, informed atheists) might conclude that 1) there is indeed evidence on each side, 2) the evidence must be weighed, and 3) there may be emotional factors that impact the weighing of the evidence.[2]

The phenomenon of brilliant believers surely figures into a cumulative case for theism. So if I were to examine the former 16 lines of evidence and draw a firm conclusion that there is a God, but there were no serious intellectuals who held this opinion, I'd have reason to seriously question my reasoning. But if a strong cadre of intellectuals agreed with me, I'd at least feel that I'm reasoning on a level playing field.

In contrast to the God question, flying spaghetti monsters are not regularly discussed by today's top intellects in a steady stream of peer-reviewed journals and Oxford University Press books. This data at the very least gives contrary evidence for the contention that all believers are either uninformed or deluded.

So how do you rate this line of evidence? It's certainly not convincing, if taken by itself. But for many it adds weight to a cumulative case. How do you rate it?

Not convincing at all – 0 1 2 3 4 5 6 7 8 9 10 - Totally Convincing

For Further Seeking

Tihomir Dimitrov compiled and commented on a list of great believers who distinguished themselves in various fields, including literature and peace efforts. It's titled *50 Nobel Laureates and Other Great Scientists Who Believe in God*, and is available as a free ebook here: http://nobelists.net . Roy Abraham Varghese introduces us to a variety of intellectual believers in *The Intellectuals Speak Out about God*. Henry Schaefer's book, *Science and Christianity: Conflict and Coherence*, provides not only his personal search for God (Chapter 9), but also lists many groundbreaking scientists who talk about their religious faith (Chapter 2). To find some of his talks free online, see http://www.leaderu.com/offices/schaefer/lectures.html .

Eric Barrett and David Fisher's *Scientists Who Believe* allows 21 scientists to tell their own stories.

Exhibit 18

Objections to Theism Aren't Insurmountable

Dr. Marilyn McCord Adams (1943-)
Distinguished Research Professor of Philosophy, Rutgers University
Researching/Writing on The Problem of Evil

So far, I've solely given evidence for theism. But what if there are strong arguments against theism, either defeaters that show theism to be logically absurd, or evidence against God's existence that demonstrates that He almost certainly can't exist?

The Problem of Evil

Some have proposed that the problem of evil is a defeater for theism. After all, if God is all good, He wouldn't want evil and suffering in the world. If God is all powerful, He could eliminate evil from the world. If He is all wise, He would know how to eliminate evil. Yet, evil exists. Thus, conclude some, an all-good, all-powerful, all-wise God must not exist.

But the problem of evil, at best, seems to call into question one or more of the traditional *attributes* of God, such as his absolute goodness, not the *existence* of God. And it's logically possible that God has good reasons to allow suffering and evil. As agnostic philosopher Dr. Paul Draper at Purdue University puts it concerning the problem of evil:

> "Logical arguments from evil are a dying (dead?) breed . . . . For all we know, even an omnipotent and omniscient being might be forced to allow [evil] for the sake of obtaining some important good. Our knowledge of goods and evils and the logical relations they have to each other is much too limited to prove that this could not be the case."[1]

Since this book deals with God's *existence* rather than his moral character, I'll refer readers to the recommended authors below to see how they handle God's goodness. It certainly doesn't appear that the problem of evil presents a defeater for all conceptions of God.

Dawkins' Challenge to Theism: Is a Complicated God Highly Unlikely?

Richard Dawkins claims to have a defeater for theism—at least an argument that makes God's existence highly unlikely. In chapter four of *The God Delusion* Dawkins argues that if God's smart enough and powerful enough to create a complicated universe, then He Himself must be extremely complicated. So the odds that something as complicated as a God could have evolved into existence through natural processes seems pretty remote. And if you claim that He was created by another intelligent being, you have to ask who made that being, and end up in an infinite regress. Thus, it's highly unlikely that God exists, according to Dawkins.[2]

But Dawkins seems to forget that few if any serious theists believe in an evolved or created God. As such, he fails to mount an argument against a God *who exists eternally outside space and time*. In other words, Dawkins seems to have erected and knocked down a straw man, or in this case a straw God. As academic biologist H. Allen Orr noted in his *New York Review of Books* discussion of *The*

God Delusion, this argument against God's existence was "shredded by reviewers."[3]

So if I'm right that no strong defeaters of theism exist, we're back to simply evaluating lines of evidence for God's existence.

For Further Seeking

Concerning the practical problem of evil, I like Phillip Yancey, a great contemporary thinker and writer, who wrote *Where is God When It Hurts?* In *Sometimes Mountains Move,* former Surgeon General C. Everett Koop reflects spiritually upon his son's death on a mountain-climbing expedition. C.S. Lewis wrote the now classic, *The Problem with Pain.* See also *A Grief Observed*, where Lewis reflected upon the death of his wife by cancer. For a professional philosopher who's written much on the problem of evil, consider Marilyn McCord Adams (having taught at Rutgers, Yale, Oxford, etc.).

For a great overview of the deeper philosophical ruminations on the problem of evil, see this article (http://plato.stanford.edu/entries/evil/) in the online *Stanford Encyclopedia of Philosophy*.

Concerning Dawkins' argument, I deal with it in more depth in my book, *Richard Dawkins and His God Delusion*. H. Allen Orr's critique of Dawkins' argument can be found in the *New York Review of Books*, "A Mission to Convert" (Jan. 11, 2007).

Exhibit 19

Positive Arguments for Naturalism Don't Prevail Over Arguments for God's Existence

Thomas Nagel (1937-)
Professor of Philosophy and Law Emeritus at New York University

Arguments for Naturalism

"But the approach of this book isn't fair," one might object. "You've listed positive arguments for theism, but none for naturalism. What if naturalism has knockdown, drag out arguments in its favor?"

Typically, I don't find atheists forwarding positive arguments for naturalism. If a positive argument is presented, it might boil down to: "A lot of things have been shown to be explained by purely natural processes. Therefore, we should expect that everything has a natural explanation, even if we have yet to find it."

Yet, the observation that "a lot of things have been shown to be explained by purely natural processes" is perfectly consistent with theism, which only claims that "*certain* data (such as miracles or the origin of the universe) are better explained by supernatural causes."

Thus, many naturalists deny that they need to defend naturalism. It's simply their default stance until they see sufficient evidence for supernaturalism. (Thus the approach of this book.)

Another interesting point in this discussion is that, in theory, naturalism can't be proven with any degree of assurance. The best a naturalist can say is that "I have yet to find strong evidence of a supernatural event." But who knows...he might find that evidence tomorrow via a dramatic experience or exploring a new line of evidence.

This is precisely what occurred to Peter Hitchens when he saw the religious painting of the afterlife. He realized that as a naturalist he couldn't know, with any degree of assurance, whether or not there were people consciously existing in an afterlife. He asked himself, "And what if there were? How did I know there were not? I did not know. I could not know."[1] In other words, he knew no defeaters of the afterlife hypothesis, so he couldn't rule it out.

Are There Problems with Naturalism?

Some atheists/agnostics don't agree that we should assume naturalism. They see inherent problems with it. (Of course, all the lines of argument presented in this book, if sound and valid, are problems with naturalism! But it's interesting that some atheists see problems with naturalism as well.)

Atheist Thomas Nagel, professor at New York University, no longer considers himself a naturalist. How's that? In his book *Mind and Cosmos*, he argues that naturalism fails to explain such obvious features as minds and consciousness. Since he's not comfortable with theism as an alternative, he proposes that perhaps someone will come up with a hypothesis that's neither naturalistic nor theistic.

The Bottom Line

I don't see an argument for naturalism that's strong enough to be a defeater for theism. Thus, we don't have to explain away the large number of naturalistic events in order to search for God. Theism is comfortable with most events in life puttering along naturalistically.

For Further Searching

Of course, any of the books recommended in the 17 lines of evidence would give greater insight into problems with naturalism. In this exceptional blog post, a former naturalist comments on a large number of books that convinced him that naturalism ultimately fails.
http://bleedingheartlibertarians.com/2013/10/contemporary-christian-philosophy-a-primer/ .
An additional book that I've not personally read, but comes highly recommended, is *Irreducible Mind: Toward a Psychology for the 21st Century*, by Edward F. Kelley, et. al., 2009. It's an 800 page tome that Harvard neurologist Eben Alexander recommends "for those still stuck in the trap of scientific skepticism." Also, check out Nagel's *Mind & Cosmos*.

Exhibit 20
"Pascal's Wager" Suggests that Fence-Sitters Bet on God

Blaise Pascal (1623-1662)
Sculpture Titled "Cycloid," by Augustin Pajou, 1785, at the Louvre

Pascal and His Wager

Let's imagine that your calculations tallied up to all zeroes except for one five. In other words, at least one line of evidence brings you to the 50/50 mark for believing in God. You're an agnostic.

"After all," you reason, "huge amounts of ink have been spilled by capable intellectuals on both sides of the many lines of evidence. How could anyone, with finality, prove or disprove God's existence? I see evidence on both sides. Yet, I still have to decide how I will live my life. I either go to church or don't. I either pray and/or meditate or I don't. I either encourage my children to live a religious life or I don't. I either live by a certain set of religious principles, or I don't."

Scientist/mathematician/philosopher Blaise Pascal (it's surely relevant that he helped develop probability theory), suggested that the wise fence-sitter should "bet" on God, living as if He exists.

Realizing that my present deeds and attitudes toward God might indeed impact my afterlife, I have extra motivation to live a useful life, such as helping the less fortunate, and will probably, in many ways, live a happier life because of it. When I die, even if God didn't exist, I lost little by living for Him. I'd simply rot in the grave like everyone else. (Of course, the gain/loss ratio would vary depending upon the context, such as those living in cultures where believers are severely persecuted.)

Yet, if I wager *against* God and live as if He doesn't exist, I take a huge risk, since this might very well negatively impact my happiness in the afterlife.

A Contemporary Example of Risk Management

Imagine that you live in New Orleans. Fifty percent of the weather experts are predicting that a devastating hurricane will hit squarely on your beach in two days, almost assuredly demolishing your house and submerging it in water. The other fifty percent predict that other factors will cause the hurricane to veer east on the last day, sparing New Orleans.

Meteorologists are divided, but you must make a decision. Wait another day and the traffic may make leaving impossible. What do you do?

Those who specialize in assessing risk would suggest that you live *as if the storm will hit*. With a 50/50 chance, the risk is too great to chance it. Board up the house, rent a vehicle to carry your valuables, and travel with your family out of harm's way.

The great French skeptic Voltaire understood risk management. Although he'd delighted skeptical readers for decades with his criticism of religion, when he got closer to death, he got in good standing with the Catholic Church, just in case he was wrong.

Betting as Seeking

Participating in religious rituals you only halfway believe in may at first sound hypocritical. But Pascal believed it was a part of sincere seeking. Think back to Exhibit 10, which explored pragmatism as an approach to discovering truth. By practicing a religious course, you get to "taste and see" if it works. By praying, you just might get an answer. By meditating, you just might connect with something beyond the natural.

Thus scientist Henry Schaefer participated in religious practices *as a part of his search*. He didn't grow up reading the Bible, so he started reading a chapter a day. He chose churches to attend wherever he lived. If he got turned off to a church, he visited others. And he learned from intelligent believers he met there.

[Running this argument in terms of *potential risk* (the hurricane) puts it in a rather negative light, as if religious decisions are all about fear. If that's a turn off, try running the argument in terms of *potential reward.* Many people put money into lotteries for a long shot at a huge potential reward. In our example, where a person is already at a 50/50 position (agnostic), the potential for reward would be quite high for betting on God, especially compared to a lottery.]

So it's decision time concerning Pascal's Wager. Is it convincing? Or was Pascal missing something? Should agnostics live as though God exists?

To Continue Your Search

Pascal laid out his wager in section 233 of his collection of thoughts, titled *Pensées* (available free online). The online Stanford Encyclopedia of Philosophy has a great introductory article titled "Pascal's Wager," which includes 65+ references to articles/books on the subject. Google "Risk Theory" and "Decision Theory" to see how these contemporary fields, used practically by businesses and governments, impact our assessments of risk.

Conclusion
Tallying Up Your Cumulative Case

So where do you presently stand on the God question? How do you tally up your conclusions on each line of argument?

Why a "6" on Even One Argument May Make You a Believer

The argument for belief in God seems to be what philosophers and scientists call a "black swan" argument. Europeans once believed that all swans were white, since they'd seen thousands of white swans and assumed that no black swans existed. Yet, one day a European travelled to Australia and observed a black swan. The evidence that he had indeed seen a black swan was enough to topple the evidence of people who had seen only white swans so far in life.

Similarly, if the claim that "nothing supernatural exists" is based exclusively on the observation that "many things have been shown to have purely natural causes," then it should take only one event with sufficient evidence of a supernatural cause to counter that claim. That event could be a near-death experience or waking in the night to strongly sense the presence of a distant loved one, presumed to be healthy, but who passed away at that exact moment. It could be a sustained reflection on the astronomical odds of incredibly complex living cells coming about by blind, natural processes.

Again, I don't necessarily need a dozen arguments to convince me that God and the afterlife exist. One compelling argument just might do, and in the cases of many brilliant skeptics who became believers, one primary event or line of argument often sufficed to induce the paradigm shift. (E.g., Antony Flew contemplating the DNA evidence; Mortimer Adler had an unusual encounter in the hospital; Bill Wilson had a dramatic answer to prayer.)

How Additional Lines of Evidence Build a Stronger Case

If you rate only one argument with a 6, even if all other arguments ranked 0, you seem to be concluding that it's more likely than not that God exists. You're a tentative theist, yet still teetering on the line between theism and agnosticism. Yet, if you give some weight to other arguments, they can provide further support for that argument and might result in a greater *cumulative impact*.

Mutually Supporting Arguments

Imagine that your study of near-death experiences convinces you that people are truly experiencing a supernatural aspect of reality. You give it a probability of 6. But note that NDErs often claim that they experienced a "Being of Light" *in a place devoid of time and in which the restrictions of space/distance didn't seem to apply.*

So when the believer in NDEs contemplates the beginning of the universe, he may have no problem positing an eternal God who exists *outside time and space* as the most reasonable cause. For him, something existing outside time and space was made more plausible by his study of NDEs. Consequently, his tentative (just a 6) belief in NDEs makes the cosmological argument more plausible.

He may reason: "Since it seems highly unlikely that something can come out of nothing, it makes more sense that *something* jumpstarted the universe. I'll place my bet on that "being of light" that people talk about in their near-death experiences."

In this way, the corroborating evidence that personal beings are living in a dimension void of space and time makes it more plausible that a God existing outside space and time caused the Big Bang. For that reason, he may rate the beginning of the universe a 7 rather than the 6 he would have assigned it had he never heard of NDEs.

And when this same person, now armed with a belief in a "personal being of light who probably created the universe," contemplates a miracle story from a trusted relative, he weighs the evidence without a prior commitment to naturalism. To him, it's certainly plausible that a personal God (as described by NDErs) would occasionally work miracles, so he tries to objectively weigh the evidence for each miracle claim, rather than always assuming naturalistic outliers or accusing the person of employing "God of the Gaps." Instead, he weighs the evidence and gives his friend's claimed miracle claim a "7."

Now let's imagine that you see loopholes in all the other lines of evidence, assessing them to be essentially worthless. You give these remaining arguments all zeroes.

How to Tally Up Your Personal Valuation of the Current State of the Evidence

So how do you tally all this up? Not by taking an average of all the arguments, since the zeroes don't count against your evidence. If you deemed an argument from personal religious experiences a 0, you've simply judged that argument to be very poor. Neither do you take an average of your positive counts (as if a 6, 7, and 8 would result in a 7), since the lower numbers don't take away from your larger numbers.

Basically, you have three lines of argument, each deemed as giving sufficient evidence (more likely than not) for the existence of God. One yielded a 6, another a 7, and another an 8. In this case, your present level of belief in the supernatural would be at least an 8, because one of the lines of evidence yielded an 8. But I say "at least," because these three "more likely than not" lines of evidence just might combine to yield a greater certainty, perhaps a 9 or even a 10.

A Helpful Analogy

Imagine yourself in a jury. A seemingly reliable eyewitness claimed to have seen the defendant with the stolen object (yielding a 6 out of 10); the defendant had a motive for the theft (yielding a 7); and he was seen at the crime scene (yielding an 8). While each of these independently yields no more than an 8 out of 10 degree of certainty, taking them together (building the case) may yield a degree of certainty of 9. That's the nature of a cumulative case.

Time to Tally up Your Numbers!

So look back over your numbers for each line of argument and try to estimate where you currently stand, taking into account the cumulative impact of each argument.

Not convincing at all – 0 1 2 3 4 5 6 7 8 9 10 – Totally Convincing

Epilogue
The Priority of the Search

So you've tallied up your tentative conclusion, based upon what is perhaps your first exposure to the evidence. If you're like me, the books and experiences of my teen years were just the beginning of my God search. One line of argument may have whet your appetite to read further. You may, following Dr. Schaefer's lead, read religious texts and attend religious services at a variety of places of worship. Perhaps you'll seek through prayer or meditation.

From my experience, it's the ultimate challenge, and well worth the effort. Happy God hunt!

Appendix 1
Additional Lines of Evidence

I introduced 17 lines of evidence. There are many more; some I've explored, others I know only by name. Alvin Plantinga (Notre Dame, retired) suggests two dozen or so arguments that he believes have merit in a set of unedited lecture notes.

(https://www.calvin.edu/academic/philosophy/virtual_library/articles/plantinga _alvin/two_dozen_or_so_theistic_arguments.pdf)

Search in Google for "Alvin Plantinga, two dozen or so theistic arguments" for the free .pdf.

The ontological argument, first formulated by Anselm of Canterbury in 1078, continues to enamor philosophers with contemporary makeovers.

Presuppositionalists insist that there are no neutral facts; we see all data through our glasses, which are colored by our worldviews. Thus, they argue that only by starting with (presupposing) a Christian worldview can we have a basis for the scientific method, rationality, and other methods/values/purposes/etc. that we deem central to life. (The present book argues primarily from an *evidential*, as opposed to *presuppositional* approach.)

Philosophers Alvin Plantinga, Nicholas Wolterstorff (Yale University), and William Alston (Syracuse University, deceased) are/were proponents of Reformed Epistemology, which asserts "that ordinary religious experiences of awe, gratitude, contrition, etc., ground the beliefs implied by the believer's sincere reports of such experiences, provided they can be said to cause those beliefs. Such grounded beliefs are warranted provided they can be defended against known objections. They can then be used as evidence for further religious beliefs."[1]

Some marshal evidence that supernatural forces of evil exist. Others argue that spiritual gifts, such as prophecy or speaking in ecstatic or unlearned languages, point to a divine cause. Still others employ historical methods to argue that God has revealed Himself at certain points in history, such as in the life of Christ.

The readings suggested in Appendix 2 will expand upon various approaches to philosophy of religion and apologetics.

Appendix 2
For Further Study and Research

1. Entry Level Resources. If you're new to philosophy of religion, start here.

a. Go back and look at my recommended readings at the end of each chapter.

b. Dr. William Lane Craig, an academic specialist in philosophy of religion, has a helpful short list of suggested readings, (http://www.reasonablefaith.org/christian-apologetics-books) helpfully tagged as Beginner, Intermediate, and Advanced.

http://www.reasonablefaith.org/christian-apologetics-books

c. This list (http://www.apologetics315.com/2009/11/recommended-apologetics-book-directory.html) also helps to distinguish between beginner and advanced books.

http://www.reasonablefaith.org/christian-apologetics-books

2. Advanced Resources. These resources typically require some background in philosophy and/or strong motivation. To lead you to these academic resources, I recommend two free, online, peer-reviewed encyclopedias. They provide balanced articles on various related issues (e.g. articles on "theism," "miracles," etc.) and recommended books under each article. Appealing to serious and more advanced students, they won't typically recommend entry level ("popular") books. Recommendations will be biased toward academic journals and academic presses (such as Oxford University Press). Advantage: articles and recommended books tend to be up-to-date and authoritative.

- The Stanford Encyclopedia of Philosophy
- The Internet Encyclopedia of Philosophy

3. Peer-Reviewed Journals Covering Philosophy of Religion

Here are a handful of often-recommended journals:

- _Faith and Philosophy_ (Associated with the Society of Christian Philosophers, Asbury Theological Seminary, and Georgetown University)
- _International Journal for Philosophy of Religion_ (Incorporates issues of _Ars Disputandi_ as well, published by the academic publisher Springer)
- _Philosophia Christi_ (Associated with the Evangelical Philosophical Society and Biola University)
- _Religious Studies_ (Subtitled: _An International Journal for the Philosophy of Religion_, Cambridge University Press)
- _Sophia_ (Published by Springer)

Here is a list of about 30 journals (including the above) in the field. It's maintained by Wesley J. Wildman, a philosophy professor at Boston University.

http://philosophyofreligion.org/?page_id=488

Acknowledgements

I want to acknowledge so many professors, who, in both religious and secular institutions, taught me how to think. Especially impactful have been Dr. Robertson McQuilkin, Dr. Albert McAllister, Dr. William Lane Craig, and Dr. Stuart Hackett. Thanks also for the thousands of authors who've influenced me through their writings.

Thanks also for those who took time to read earlier versions of the manuscript and gave input. Kennesaw State University student Jonathan Mann should especially be singled out for his many insights and recommended resources. Also, thanks for input from students in my Introduction to the Study of Religion class. Thanks also to early readers Eric Mattson, Dr. Gene Williams, and family members Richard and Ann.

Thanks especially to my dear wife Cherie, who endures endless conversations about such matters, recommending relevant articles and constantly impacting the development of my thinking.

Endnotes

Introduction for Teachers

1. Here's a brief introductory article–*Why Study Religion?*–*on the University of Pennsylvania site:* https://www.sas.upenn.edu/religious_studies/why-study-religion . I assign it to my Introduction to Religion students to motivate them, help them reflect on their own motivations, and to take the class more seriously.

2. Richard Dawkins, in *The God Delusion*, defines a "delusion" as "a persistent false belief held in the face of strong contradictory evidence," claiming that this "captures religious faith perfectly." (Great Britain: Bantam Press, 2006), p. 28.

3. Mallory Nye, *Religion: The Basics* (Routledge, second edition, 2008), p. 4.

4. The text I refer to is Edward Craig, *Philosophy: A Brief Insight* (New York: Sterling, 2002). Out of his eight total chapters, a full chapter was dedicated to explaining and reinforcing Hume's *Of Miracles*. The following chapter, rather than providing any critique of Hume, or laying out a contemporary argument for the existence of God, moves on to other matters. Many Introduction to Philosophy syllabi I find online seem follow this same path: students read Hume, then move past the God issue, implying that all rational discussion of God's existence ended with Hume.

5. *Of Miracles* came under heavy fire by Hume's contemporaries. Recent critiques of Hume include respected philosopher John Earman (himself being apparently an agnostic), in *Hume's Abject Failure* (Oxford University Press, 2000) and Craig S. Keener, *Miracles* (Baker Academic, 2011), pp. 107-208.

6. The one in 25 statistic is cited by Pim van Lommel, *Consciousness Beyond Life* (New York: HarperCollins, 2010), p. 9. In Australia, a telephone survey of 673 people found nine percent claiming to have experienced a near-death experience. M. Perera, et al., Prevalence of Near-Death Experiences in Australia, *Journal of Near-Death Studies*, 24 (2) (2005), 109-115.

7. Cheryl L. Nosek, Christopher W. Kerr, et. al., "End-of-Life Dreams and Visions: A Qualitative Perspective from Hospice Patients," *American Journal of Hospice & Palliative Medicine*, 2015, Vol. 32(3) 269-274. See also Christopher W. Kerr, James P. Donnelly, et. al., End-of-Life Dreams and Visions: A Longitudinal Study of Hospice Patients' Experiences, *Journal of Palliative Medicine*, Volume 17, Number 3, 2014. This was the first study to actually interview the dying on a regular basis, asking them if they'd had any unusual dreams or visions. Before this study, typically nurses and others were interviewed about their experiences with the dying, yielding percentages of patients experiencing deathbed visions at about 30 percent of all patients. [See Muthumana, Meena Kumari, et. al., "Deathbed Visions from India: A Study of Family Observations in Northern Kerala," *Omega*, vol. 62 (2), pp. 97-109, 2010-2011.] Thus, going straight to the dying patients yielded a much higher percentage. Apparently, many dying people are reluctant to share these experiences, if they're not directly asked.

8. According to Craig S. Keener, *Miracles* (Grand Rapids: Baker Academic, 2011), p. 204, citing a Pew survey.

9. For a good overview of this renaissance, see "Modernizing the Case for God," *Time* (7 April 1980), pp. 65-66.

See also, William Lane Craig, The Revolution in Anglo-American Philosophy: How the field of philosophy has experienced a Christian renaissance over the last half century. To see the revolution from the perspective of a respected naturalistic philosopher, see Quentin Smith, The Metaphilosophy of Naturalism, *Philo*, Fall/Winter, 2001, Vol 4, no. 2, pp. 195-215.

10. The Metaphilosophy of Naturalism, opt. cit., p. 197. The Oxford University Press catalog he referred to was the 2000-2001 edition.

11. When I asked my students what they wanted to cover in our "Introduction to the Study of Religion" class, the existence of God was one of the main topics they suggested.

Introduction for Students

1. Richard Dawkins, *The God Delusion* (New York: Houghton Mifflin, 2008), p. 346.

2. Ibid., p. 83. In an interview, he put it even stronger: "no shred of evidence."

3. While some religious believers may define faith in this way, that's certainly not how faith is defined in the primary documents of the Christian faith. Rather, in multiple contexts, they encourage intelligent examination of their claims. (See I Peter 3:15, Romans 1:20, Acts 2:22, I Peter 1:16, John 5:31, John 20:24-31, Acts 1:3, etc.) The authoritative dictionaries of the Greek New Testament, (e.g., Baur, Arndt and Gingrich; Colin Brown, etc.), which derive their definitions from a careful study of the documents in the original Greek language, never define "faith" as "belief without evidence." Rather, they define it as "belief, trust, or confidence"; a belief or confidence which, in numerous contexts, is claimed to be based upon evidence as opposed to a blind leap.

4. Francis Collins, *The Language of God* (New York: Simon & Schuster, 2006), p. 16.

5. Ibid, pp. 8-31.

6. In the Christian faith, it's those who sincerely and *continuously* (the impact of the Greek present tense) seek and ask who will find ultimate truth. (Matthew 7:7,8)

7. A good example may be the world's most famous atheist, Richard Dawkins, who as a 17-year-old believed in the existence of God, but based this belief solely upon the strength of the argument from design. (And, he adds, because his musical hero Elvis believed in God.) But one of his friends convinced him that a thorough understanding of Darwin made the argument from design passé. Thus, when this one argument fell, Dawkins embraced atheism. *Richard Dawkins: An Appetite for Wonder* (New York: HarperCollins, 2013), pp. 139-142.

8. Atheist Susan Blackmore, in studying near-death experiences, called the two hypotheses the "Afterlife Hypothesis" and the "Dying Brain Hypothesis." *Dying to Live* (Buffalo: Prometheus Books, 1993), pp. 3, 4.

9. Gardner Murphy, Robert O. Ballou, *William James on Psychical Research* (Viking Press, 1960), p. 41. As an example, Antony Flew (1923-2010) was one of, if not *the* most influential atheistic philosopher of his time. He shocked the world by announcing, in his later years, that he'd come to believe in God. In his book, *There Is a God*, he cited his reason for shifting positions: "almost entirely because of the DNA investigations." (p. 75) I quote him more extensively in Exhibit 8.

10. Study "motivated reasoning."

Exhibit 1
Near-Death Experiences

1. Pim van Lommel, et al., "Near-death experience in survivors of cardiac arrest: a prospective study in the Netherlands," *The Lancet*, Volume 358 , Issue 9298 , 2039-2045.

2. Pim van Lommel, *Consciousness Beyond Life* (New York: HarperCollins, 2010).

3. Ibid., p. 9. An Australian telephone survey of 673 people found nine percent claiming to have NDEs. M. Perera, et al., Prevalence of Near-Death Experiences in Australia, *Journal of Near-Death Studies*, 24 (2) 2005), 109-115.

4. Van Lommel lists 12 NDE elements. Ibid., pp. 17-41. See also J. Steve Miller, *Near-Death Experiences as Evidence for the Existence of God and Heaven* (Acworth, GA: Wisdom Creek Press, 2012), pp. 25-29.

5. Van Lommel's study was longitudinal, repeating the interviews at various intervals. See especially pp. 45ff.

6. On "contrary to expectations," see Raymond A. Moody, *Life After Life* (New York: Bantam Books, 1975), p. 175. See also J. Steve Miller, opt. cit., pp. 57-60. On similarities across cultures, see J. Steve Miller, pp. 95-103.

7. This remarkable NDE was researched and reported by Dr. Michael Sabom in his book, *Light & Death* (Grand Rapids: Zondervan Publishing House, 1998), pp. 37-47; 184-190.

8. These have consistently been the results I've seen of well-done, recent work summarizing the peer-reviewed literature on NDEs. The following books did an especially good job of reviewing the literature: J.M. Holden, B. Greyson, D. James, *The Handbook of Near-Death Experiences: Thirty Years of Investigation* (Santa Barbara, California: ABC-CLIO, 2009); Penny Sartori, *The Near Death Experiences of Hospitalized Intensive Care Patients: A Five-Year Clinical Study* (New York: The Edwin Mellen Press, 2008).

9. I speak of these supernatural elements in J. Steve Miller, opt. cit., pp. 49-80. For references to 107 NDEs that exhibited corroboration, see Janice Miner Holden, opt. cit., Table 9.1, p. 194.

10. For a book dedicated solely to exploring and replying to the naturalistic explanations of NDEs, see Chris Carter, *Science and the Near-Death Experience* (Rochester: Inner Traditions, 2010).

11. See J. Steve Miller, opt. cit., pp. 49-80.

Exhibit 2
Deathbed Experiences

1. See this TEDx talk by Dr. Christopher W. Kerr, from his ongoing research of over 1400 dying patients, "I See Dead People: Dreams and Visions of the Dying". One benefit of watching the talk is that Kerr plays actual footage of dying people telling their stories. Rather than being drowsy and confused, they appear to be as alert and reasonable as people who aren't dying. According to Kerr, deathbed visions "are so frequent they are essentially intrinsic to the process of dying." To the patient, they are "real, intense, meaningful." http://www.nextavenue.org/not-taught-in-med-school-interpreting-dreams-of-the-dying/

2. Christopher W. Kerr, James P. Donnelly, Scott T. Wright, Sarah M. Kuszczak, Anne Banas, MD, Pei C. Grant, PhD, and Debra L. Luczkiewicz, End-of-Life Dreams and Visions: A Longitudinal Study of Hospice Patients' Experiences, *Journal of Palliative Medicine*, Volume 17, Number 3, 2014, pp. 301,302.

3. Sir William Barrett, *Death-bed Visions* (London: Methuen, 1926, reprinted in 2011), pp. 11-14. Barrett was a pioneering scientist who taught physics at the Royal College of Science in Dublin. Barrett's collection of deathbed visions was published after his death, unedited and unfinished. Yet it's interesting in that he takes each case and subjects it to scrutiny, trying to weigh the evidence for and against possible naturalistic explanations. He concluded that these were truly transitions to the other side. Osis and Haraldsson's work was a very detailed and objective study, done with modern survey methods and assessment techniques. The two studies/presentations are very different; but I found both to be valuable. Karlis Osis and Erlendur Haraldsson, *At the Hour of Death: A New Look at Evidence for Life after Death*, (White Crow Books: 2012).

4. While former studies interviewed nurses and family members about their experiences with the dying, reporting about 1/3 of dying patients telling them of deathbed experiences, this more recent study actually interviewed the dying patients. This achieved a far higher percentage of reports. Apparently, many dying people were having vivid experiences, but not telling any of the living, perhaps for fear of ridicule, or assuming that the experiences were meant only for them. This recent study is was very well done and is reported in two journal articles. The first is: Cheryl L. Nosek, Christopher W. Kerr, Julie Woodworth, Scott T. Wright, Pei C. Grant, Sarah M. Kuszczak, Anne Banas, Debra L. Luczkiewicz, and Rachel M. Depner, End-of-Life Dreams and Visions: A Qualitative Perspective From Hospice Patients, *American Journal of Hospice & Palliative Medicine*, 2015, Vol. 32(3) 269-274. The second is End-of-Life Dreams and Visions: A Longitudinal Study of Hospice Patients' Experiences, opt. cit.

5. Interesting outcomes of the India study include: 1) They had no reports of Yamadoots (a personality in Hindu literature/religion that accompanies people to the place of the dead). 2) Some predicted their own death was eminent, even when they otherwise seemed healthy. 3) One was a 9-year-old with AIDS. Studies of the young often bring out interesting perspectives, since they're not as informed by culture. 4) About 30% of 104 shared of their deathbed experience. 4) They were almost all Muslims and Hindus. 5) Typically they saw a deceased family member, who explained that they were there to accompany them to the other side.

6. These conclusions were reached by Osis and Haraldsson, as laid out in their book *At the Hour of Death*, opt. cit. See especially their summaries at the end of each chapter, and chapters 13, 14, Epilogue, and additional comments in the final section: "Evidence for Life after Death."

7. See both Christopher Kerr studies, opt. cit.

Exhibit 3
Contemporary Miracles and Answers to Prayer

1. A.E. Hotchner, *Papa Hemingway* (New York: Bantam Books, 1966), p. 55.

2. Craig S. Keener, *Miracles* (Grand Rapids: Baker Academic, 2011), pp. 204,205.

3. Invoking "God of the Gaps" seems to me, in many cases, an overused way to excuse oneself from taking the time to seriously investigate miraculous claims. Example: You ask God for something and receive it immediately: "It's just God of the Gaps!" Your best friend tells you of meeting God in a near-death experience: "It's just God of the Gaps! We just have yet to figure out the naturalistic explanation!" It appears that "God of the Gaps" is often used merely as a faith statement proclaiming that naturalism will one day explain everything, based loosely upon the fact that many events have indeed been shown to be sufficiently explained naturalistically.

4. Keener, opt. cit., p. 264.

Exhibit 4
Special Knowledge through Spiritual Encounters

1. Kevin Nelson, *The Spiritual Doorway in the Brain* (New York: Penguin, 2011), pp. 148, 211, 212.

2. See Eric C. Barrett and David Fisher, *Scientists Who Believe*, (Chicago: Moody Press, 1984), pp. 5,6, for a top Soviet physicist, Boris P. Dotsenko, who grew up a convinced atheist, but reflected upon the second law of thermodynamics and thought through the implications. "As I thought about all of that, it suddenly dawned on me that there must be a very powerful *organizing* force counteracting this disorganizing tendency within nature, keeping the universe controlled and in order. This force must be nonmaterial; otherwise, it too would become disordered. I concluded that this power must be both omnipotent and omniscient: there must be a God–one God–controlling everything!"

Exhibit 5
The Beginning of the Universe

1. According to Richard Dawkins, "The standard model of our universe says that time itself began in the big bang, along with space, some 13 billion years ago." *The God Delusion* (New York: Houghton Mifflin, 2008), p. 174.

2. Arvind Borde, Alan Guth, Alexander Vilenkin. See an interesting article on this here: http://now.tufts.edu/articles/beginning-was-beginning .

3. As physicist Paul Davies states, "The universe cannot have existed for ever, otherwise it would have reached its equilibrium end state an infinite time ago. Conclusion: the universe did not always exist." (*God and the New Physics,* 1983, p. 11.

4. Alexander Vilenkin, *Many Worlds in One* (New York: Hill and Wang, 2006), p.176. Read a nice summary article here: http://www.reasonablefaith.org/contemporary-cosmology-and-the-beginning-of-the-universe#ixzz3wHSftLds . See also "Why physicists can't avoid a creation event," by Lisa Grossman, *New Scientist* (January 11, 2012), and a video at http://www.youtube.com/watch?v=NXCQelhKJ7A . Vilenkin concludes in the video: "there are no models at this time that provide a satisfactory model for a universe without a beginning." See also Audrey Mithani, Alexander Vilenkin, "Did the universe have a beginning?" Institute of Cosmology, Department of Physics and Astronomy, Tufts University, April 20, 2012.

5. Francis Collins, *The Language of God* (New York: Simon & Schuster, 2006), p. 67.

6. Henry F. Schaefer, *Science and Christianity: Conflict or Coherence?* (Watkinsville, GA: The Apollos Trust, 2003), p. 75.)

7. Jana Harmon, *Atheist Conversions to Christianity*, a presentation of her PhD research at the University of Birmingham, England. https://www.youtube.com/watch?v=EemxEK9TtEo

Exhibit 6
Six Super-Precise Numbers
That Fine-Tune our Universe for Life

1. Richard Dawkins writes of the settings of the strong force in *The God Delusion* (New York: Houghton Mifflin, 2008), pp. 170-180. For Martin Reese's explanation, see *Just Six Numbers* (New York: Basic Books, 1999), pp. 47-51.

2. Roger Penrose, "Time-Asymmetry and Quantum Gravity," in *Quantum Gravity* 2, ed. C.J. Isham, R. Penrose, and D.W. Sciama (Oxford: Clarendon, 1981), p. 249.

3. Neither Dawkins nor Reese find a reason a big bang should *of necessity* spit out a universe with these exact settings. Thus, they conclude that the settings were either by design (implying a Designer), or by luck. *The God Delusion*, opt. cit., p. 73. *Just Six Numbers*, opt. cit., p. 4.

4. This was from a presentation by academic physicist Eric Smith at Kennesaw State University in the Fall of 2015.

5. *Just Six Numbers, opt. cit.,* p. 157.

6. Eric Smith, in his lecture, argued that the odds for the settings by chance were inconceivably small. Someone in the audience asked, "But isn't it at least possible?" Smith replied something like, "Well sure. But it's *possible* that a fully functioning human head could pop up in the air in front of me, start talking, then disappear 10 seconds later. But the odds are so far against it that we speak of the odds practically as impossible." Thus, advocates of this argument hold that [concerning the settings of the universe] the odds of something like this happening naturalistically, by chance, is essentially what we describe as nil, or impossible.

7. http://www.reasonablefaith.org/divine-psychology#ixzz4AFNhRWbC .

Exhibit 7
The Order and Laws of our Universe

1. This was in an interview with George S. Viereck, first published as "What Life Means to Einstein," in the *Saturday Evening Post*, Oct. 26, 1929. I'm quoting secondarily from Walter Isaacson, *Einstein: His Life and Universe* (New York: Simon & Schuster, 2007) p. 386. For more on Einstein's belief in God, see Isaacson's entire chapter dedicated to this, pp. 384-393. While Dawkins argues that Einstein was a closet atheist, Isaacson disagrees, arguing 1) Einstein explicitly denied being an atheist 2) He positively claimed that he believed in God, describing God as an impersonal God 3) Einstein wasn't one to sugar-coat controversial beliefs to please people 4) Einstein said he hated it when atheists quoted him to support their views. See *Einstein* (pp. 384-393).

2. Isaac Newton, *The Mathematical Principles of Natural Philosophy* (trans. By Andrew Motte), Book III, General Scholium, section 504.

https://en.wikisource.org/wiki/The_Mathematical_Principles_of_Natural_Philosophy_%281846%29/BookIII-General_Scholium

Exhibit 8
The Vast Complexity of the Earliest Cells
The Origin of Life

1. On being dragged to his conclusion of design kicking and screaming, see Hoyle's conclusion in *Evolution from Space*. "As our ideas developed, a monstrous spectre kept beckoning." Note that it's not just a spectre; it's a "monstrous spectre." Just what was this spectre, which he'd tried so diligently to avoid? The data of his research had exhausted the productive powers of chance working in a solely naturalistic environment. The looming spectre was Intelligence. See especially pages 147-150 of *Evolution from Space*. Hoyle concludes that preexisting information–analogous to a computer or a library–is insufficient to account for the emergence of cells, since you'd still have to ask where the information/computers/libraries came from. Eventually, Hoyle concludes that the only satisfactory explanation is intelligence–something that not only *contains* information, but has the ability to *use* that information to program something.

2. Stephen C. Meyer discusses many of these estimates in chapter 9 (pp. 194-214) of *Signature in the Cell*, (New York: HarperOne, 2009). In the 1980s, MIT biochemist Robert Sauer and his team estimated that a chance assemblage of a functional sequence of an amino acid (a part of the cell) would be about one chance in 10^{63}. Cambridge Postdoctoral researcher Douglas Axe later determined that Sauer underestimated "how much protein sequences can vary and still maintain function." He reestimated taking this into account and came up with 1 chance in 10^{77} (Meyer, p. 210). But to get one functional protein would be about 1 chance in 10^{164}. (p. 212) To get all the necessary proteins for a functioning cell multiplies out to 1 chance in $10^{41,000}$, very close to Hoyle's 1983 estimate. (p. 213)

3. Fred Hoyle, *The Intelligent Universe* (Holt, Rinehart and Winston, 1984).

4. Fred Hoyle, "The Universe: Past and Present Reflections," *Engineering and Science*, Volume 45:2, November, 1981, pp. 8-12.

5. Richard Dawkins, *The God Delusion* (Great Britain: Bantam Press, 2006), pp. 166,167.

6. Ibid., p. 167.

7. Ibid., p. 166.

8. Dawkins details his studies and dissertation thesis in his memoir, *Richard Dawkins, An Appetite for Wonder* (New York: HarperCollins, 2013).

9. *An Appetite for Wonder*, opt. cit., p. 291. He quotes Charles Darwin as writing that he would "never have succeeded with metaphysics or mathematics." Then Dawkins reflects, "same for me...."

10. Antony Flew, *There Is A God* (New York: HarperOne, 2007), p. 75.

11. *The God Delusion*, opt. cit., pp. 166,188,189.

12. Whereas many naturalists complain of such arguments as "God of the gaps," where God is invoked to explain data or mechanisms that can't presently be explained by science, couldn't this argument by Dawkins be called a "nature of the gaps" argument, since he insists that the naturalistic explanation always makes more sense, no matter how speculative, than a theistic explanation? All Dawkins can offer as "evidence" is to shift the numbers, or to say that he hopes that a naturalistic mechanism will one day be discovered.

Exhibit 9
The Complexity of Living Creatures

1.Michael J. Behe, *Darwin's Black Box: The Biochemical Challenge to Evolution* (New York: Free Press, 2006), p. 5.

2. Ibid., p. 39.

3. Ibid., pp. 69-73.

4. Richard Dawkins uses the arch analogy on pages 156ff of *The God Delusion* (Great Britain: Bantam Press, 2006), crediting the analogy to Scottish chemist A.G. Cairns-Smith, in his book, *Seven Clues to the Origin of Life*.

5. Denton's description of the feather, and the complexities it presents for explanation by classic Darwinism, begins on p. 202. Michael Denton, *Evolution: A Theory in Crisis* (Bethesda, Maryland: Adler & Adler, 1985), pp. 202ff.

6. Darwin emphasized this in both his first edition (at the end of his introduction) and last edition of *Origin of the Species*: "I am convinced that natural selection has been the main but not the exclusive means of modification." http://literature.org/authors/darwin-charles/the-origin-of-species/introduction.html See Stephen Jay Gould's observations on this statement in his critique of Dawkins and Dennett, "Darwinian Fundamentalism", June 12, 1997, *The New York Review of Books*.

Exhibit 10
Belief in God Seems to "Fit" Life as We Experience It,
Making Life Better

1. Psalm 34:8

2. Psalm 1

3. John 10:10

4. David G. Myers, *The Pursuit of Happiness* (New York: Avon Books, 1992), p. 183.

5. Ibid. See also Myers' book, *The American Paradox* (New Haven, Connecticut, Yale University Press, 2001), on this subject, pp. 283 and 285. A more recent large-scale study found 54 percent of spiritually devoted teens describing themselves as "very happy," contrasted with 29 percent of the spiritually disengaged. See Soul *Searching: The Religious and Spiritual Lives of American Teenagers*, by Christian Smith with Melinda Lundquist Denton (New York: Oxford University Press, 2005). See especially chapter 7: Adolescent Religion and Life Outcomes.

6. Rosenberg suggests, if his atheistic, scientistic worldview is too depressing, to take Prozac or another anti-depression drug. Alex Rosenberg, *The Atheist's Guide to Reality* (New York: W.W. Norton & Company, 2011), pp. 282, 315.

7. Rosenberg himself can't live consistently with the views he espouses, as evidenced by the contradictions within his book. Example: While he claims that we can learn nothing from history, he makes recommendations based upon what he's learned from history, such as his recommendation of taking Prozak, a recommendation presumably based upon the testimonies of those who've taken it previously. Leon Wieseltier crowns Rosenberg's book "the worst book of the year." "Washington Diarist: The Answers," *New Republic* Dec. 14, 2011. *The New York Times* published another scathing critique: Philip Kitcher, "Seeing Is Unbelieving," (March 23, 2012).

8. C.S. Lewis, *Surprised by Joy* (Harcourt, Brace, Jonovich, 1966). As Frederick Nietzsche noted, "He who has a why to live for can bear almost any how." A problem with Rosenberg's worldview

is that it leaves us with no "why" to live for.

9. On the importance of using emotional intelligence in research and reasoning, see chapter 25 of J. Steve Miller and Cherie K. Miller, *Why Brilliant People Believe Nonsense* (Acworth, Georgia: Wisdom Creek Academic, 2015), pp. 366-387.

Exhibit 11
Many Attest to Sensing a God-shaped Vacuum
That Could Only Be Filled with God

1. Augustine, *The Confessions of Saint Augustine*, Book 1 (AD 401). E. B. Pusey's translation reads "Thou awakest us to delight in Thy praise; for Thou madest us for Thyself, and our heart is restless, until it repose in Thee."

2. Blaise Pascal, *Pensées* VII (425).

3. C.S. Lewis, *Mere Christianity* (New York: Macmillan Publishing Company, 1952), p. 120. To take in a bit more of the context: "Creatures are not born with desires unless satisfaction for these desires exists. A baby feels hunger: well, there is such a thing as food. A duckling wants to swim: well, there is such a thing as water. Men feel sexual desire: well, there is such a thing as sex. If I find in myself a desire which no experience in this world can satisfy, the most probable explanation is that I was made for another world. If none of my earthly pleasures satisfy it, that does not prove that the universe is a fraud. Probably earthly pleasures were never meant to satisfy it, but only to arouse it, to suggest the real thing." (*Mere Christianity*, Bk. III, chap. 10, "Hope")

4. William Craig speaks of the role of the Holy Spirit on pp. 43-51 of *Reasonable Faith* (Wheaton, Illinois: Crossway Books, Third Edition, 2008).

5. Katherine Tait, *My Father Bertrand Russell* (New York: Harcourt Brace Jovanovich, 1975).

6. Anne Rice, *Called Out of Darkness* (New York: Alfred A. Knopf, 2008).

7. Blaise Pascal, *Pensées*, section 423. Perhaps this explains why some famous atheists' children became not only religious believers, but very committed. Those brought up as atheists may feel that emptiness more than those brought up in nominal church homes. (Think: Madalyn Murray O'Hair's son, Bertrand Russell's daughter.)

8. Stephen Jay Gould, the popular science writer and Harvard professor, saw no good reason to believe in God. But he wondered at the fact that half of his intelligent colleagues were believers. Obviously, these people had reasons for their belief, but he couldn't see adequate reasons from science. He suggested that perhaps belief in God comes from a different realm of reasoning than scientific reasoning, what he called "nonoverlapping magisteria." Could "reasons of the heart" be a part of Gould's magisteria of religious belief?

Exhibit 12
Often a Paradigm Shift or Gestalt Experience
Leads to a New View of Reality

1. Thomas S. Kuhn, *The Structure of Scientific Revolutions* (Chicago and London: University of Chicago Press, 1962, 1st ed., p.44).

2. Peter Hitchens, *The Rage Against God: How Atheism Led Me to Faith* (Grand Rapids, Michigan: Zondervan, 2010), pp. 99-113.

3. Ibid., p. 12.

4. Anne Rice, *Called Out of Darkness* (New York: Alfred A. Knopf, 2008).

Exhibit 13
Such Vivid Experiences as Consciousness and Free Will
Seem to be Better Explained by the Existence of Nonmaterial Minds/Souls
That are Separate from the Brain

1. Susan Blackmore, *Dying to Live* (Buffalo, NY: Prometheus Books, 1993), pp. 136-164.
2. Alex Rosenberg, *The Atheists' Guide to Reality* (New York: W.W. Norton & Company, 2011).

Exhibit 14
Such Vivid Experiences as Objective Morals
Are Best Explained by an Objective Law–Giver

1. Immanuel Kant, *Critique of Practical Reason* (1688, 5:161.33–6; translation by Guyer 1992: 1)

Exhibit 16
Many People, of All Vocations and Levels of Education,
Report a Compelling First-Hand Experience with God

1. Mortimer J. Adler, *A Second Look in the Rearview Mirror* (Macmillan, 1992), pp. 276-278.
2. Francis Hartigan, *Bill W., A Biography of Alcoholics Anonymous Cofounder Bill Wilson* (New York: St. Martin's Press) pp. 56-69.
3. From William James' letter to a friend, quoted on the back cover of a Collier Books edition of *Varieties of Religious Experience*.

Exhibit 17
Many Respected Intellectuals Believe that Their
Line of Reasoning Is Compelling for Belief in God

1. To find more about Henry Schaefer, see his CV:
http://www.ccqc.uga.edu/people/member_page.php?id=6/ . The book I refer to is Henry F. Schaefer, *Science and Christianity: Conflict or Coherence?* (Athens, GA: The University of Georgia Printing Department, 2003).
2. On how emotional factors impact our reasoning, I found it interesting that the article on "Atheism" in the peer reviewed *Internet Encyclopedia of Philosophy* concludes, in part, that "The prospects for a simple, confined argument for atheism (or theism) that achieves widespread support or that settles the question are dim. That is because, in part, the prospects for any argument that decisively settles a philosophical question where a great deal seems to be at stake are dim."

Exhibit 18
Objections to Theism Aren't Insurmountable

1 – Daniel Howard-Snyder, editor, *The Evidential Argument from Evil* (Indiana University Press, 2008). See chapter 8 by Dr. Paul Draper, p. 151.

2 – Richard Dawkins, *The God Delusion* (Great Britain: Bantam Press, 2006). See his argument in chapter 4.

3 – H. Allen Orr's critique of Dawkins' argument can be found in the *New York Review of Books*, "A Mission to Convert" (Jan. 11, 2007).

Exhibit 19
Positive Arguments for Naturalism Don't Prevail
Over Arguments for God's Existence

1. Peter Hitchens, *The Rage Against God: How Atheism Led Me to Faith* (Grand Rapids, Michigan: Zondervan, 2010), p. 103.

Appendix

1. Forrest, Peter, "The Epistemology of Religion," *The Stanford Encyclopedia of Philosophy* (Spring 2014 Edition), Edward N. Zalta (ed.), URL = <http://plato.stanford.edu/archives/spr2014/entries/religion-epistemology/>.